JOHN SLIMICK
COMPUTER SCIENCE DEPT.
U. OF PITT AT BRADFORD
BRADFORD, PA 16701

An Introduction to
DATA STRUCTURES

An Introduction to
DATA STRUCTURES

John Beidler
University of Scranton

ALLYN AND BACON, INC.
BOSTON · LONDON · SYDNEY · TORONTO

Managing Editor: Michael E. Meehan
Production Editor: Lorraine Perrotta

Library of Congress Cataloging in Publication Data

Beidler, John, 1941–
    An introduction to data structures.

    Bibliography: p.
    Includes index.
    1. Data structures (Computer science) I. Title.
QA76.9.D35B43   001.64   81-20638
ISBN 0-205-07711-0   AACR2

Printed in the United States of America.
10 9 8 7 6 5 4 3 2   87 86 85 84 83 82

to my parents,

and my children,

but especially for my wife, Pat.

Contents

Preface   xi

1 Introduction to Data Structures   1

1. Logical Structures vs. Physical Structures   1
2. Some Data Structures   3
3. Trade Offs   5
4. Pointers   8
5. Exercises   10

2 Program Measurement   15

1. Space and Time Measurement   15
2. Timing Fundamentals   22
3. Timing Techniques — Graphing   24
4. Timing Techniques — Series Summation and Calculus   27
5. Getting a Handle on Timing   28
6. Recognizing Certain Timings   30
7. Exercises   35

3 Some Logical Structures   37

1. Sequential Structures   37
2. Sequential Structures with Very Limited Access   39
3. Graphs   42
4. Directed Graphs   44
5. Trees   45
6. Exercises   49

4 Queues and Stacks   51

1. Queues   52
2. Pushdown Stacks   55
3. Multiple Structures   60
4. Review   63
5. Exercises   64

5 Pointers and Dynamic Allocation   67

1. Memory Access   67
2. Records   68
3. Pointer Variables and Dynamic Records   70
4. A Dynamic Allocation Example   72

6 Lists   75

1. Grounded One-way Lists   75
2. Circular Lists   80
3. Two-way Linked Lists   83
4. Exercises   83

7 Trees   87

1. Binary Trees — Array Representation   87
2. Binary Trees — Record Representation   92
3. General Tree Representation   93
4. Tree Searching   97
5. Exercises   103

8 Graphs, Digraphs, and More Trees   107

1. Elementary Digraph and Graph Representations   107
2. Alternate Graph Representations   111
3. Linked Representations   114
4. Speed-Up   116
5. Some Graph Problems   117
6. AVL-Tree Restructuring   121
7. Exercises   128

9 Sorting   133

1. Selection and Exchange Methods   133
2. The Shell Sort   137
3. Quicksort and Treesort   140
4. Merging   143
5. Two Special Case Sorting Methods   149
6. Exercises   150

10 Search and Update   151

1. Sequential Search and Update   151
2. Bisection Method Search   155
3. Direct Address Search and Update   156

4. Hashing   158
5. Block Sequential Search and Update   159
6. Observations   161
7. Exercises   162

11 Recursion   163

1. Intuition and Mathematics   163
2. Fundamentals of Recursive Programming   164
3. Performing Recursion   166
4. Exercises   167

12 Storage Allocation   169

1. Dynamic Allocation — Concepts   169
2. List of Available Space   170
3. Mark/Release   174
4. Garbage Collection   175
5. Dynamic Allocation   177
6. Exercises   177

13 Some Interesting Problems   179

1. Sparse Matrices   179
2. Polynomial Arithmetic   182
3. Area of a Polygon   184
4. Cryptorythms   186
5. Error Correcting Codes   188
6. Exercises   191

14 Data Structures and Data Base Systems   193

1. Data Base Management   194
2. The Hierarchical Data Model   196
3. The Graphical Model   198
4. The Relational Model   200
5. Observations   202
6. Exercises   203

Bibliography   205

Index   211

Preface

Regardless of whether you call an undergraduate curriculum computer science, computer engineering, information systems, etc., there must be a course which emphasizes data structures. When we established our computer science curriculum we decided to place our data structures in the second semester of the sophomore year. This was done for two reasons:

1. We wished to make sure that students knew before they started their junior year what computer science was about;
2. We wanted a strong prerequisite that our upper level undergraduate courses could rely upon.

This text can be used by students with the following minimum background:

1. A modest knowledge of PASCAL;
2. A year's experience programming using structured programming techniques, preferrably in PASCAL;
3. A one semester course in assembler level programming would be preferred, but some knowledge of how computers function would be adequate;
4. Some knowledge of calculus and basic statistical concepts (median, average) is required. This could be satisfied by the typical kinds of courses normally offered for students majoring in business or the social sciences. However, students should be encouraged to go as far as they can to achieve a strong mathematics background.

The early development of this text was strongly influenced by the curriculum recommendations that appear in:

1. Curriculum '68, CACM 11,3 (March 1968), pp. 151-197;
2. The small college computer science program recommended by Austing and Engel (CACM 16,3 (March 1973), pp. 139-147);
3. The curriculum report for undergraduate programs in information systems edited by Cougar (CACM 16,12 (December 1973), pp. 727-749).

In its later stages of development, we were pleased to see how our data structures course fit in with the following curriculum recommendations:

4. Curriculum '78 - CACM 22,3 (March 1979) pp. 147-165;
5. The IEEE-Computer Society committee report on curriculum in Computer Science and Engineering (January 1977).

We believe this text is suitable for courses CS2 and CS7 in Curriculum '78, UC-1 and UC-8 in the Information Systems curriculum report, SE-2 and SE-3 from the software engineering section of the IEEE curriculum, and Course 4 in the small college program recommendations. The text was written for a one semester course in data structures. It contains material that we have taught in our sophomore level data structures course, but as with many texts this too contains too much material.

However, there is a core of material that is essential to the purpose of the text. The teacher can select other material as may be considered appropriate. The core material for each chapter is as follows:

1.   All sections, also note exercise problems 4 or 5, 6, and 7. Exercises 6 and 7 are built upon in later chapters;

2.   A difficult but important chapter that sets the tone of the text. Specifically, the techniques learned in data structures are important because of their effects upon efficient timing and space utilization. This chapter sets the framework that is built upon to measure the techniques introduced in the text. For students with minimal backgrounds, it is essential that they understand at least the purpose, if not the details of the chapter;

3.   This chapter presents the basic terminology describing the discrete structures whose various representations are built in this text. Only logical concepts are presented because we feel that the logical concepts must be understood and not confused with a particular representation. Some structures have many representations and answers to questions regarding which representation should be used might depend upon the particular application;

4.   Sections 1 and 2 must be covered. Also, the two stack representation in section 3 should be considered mandatory. The material on BUMPing and using pointers in section 3 can be briefly covered or omitted. Programming exercises should require that the students at least count the number of loop iterations and use several data sets when it is appropriate. At least simple queue problems like exercise 6 or stack problems like 4 and 5 should be assigned;

5.   This is basic material on dynamic allocation in PASCAL. This chapter should be covered completely;

6.   Sections 1 and 2 must be covered. Depending upon the time spent on earlier material, section 3 should at least be covered lightly. There are lots of good programming exercises that can be given. One of our favorites is to assign the word search problem from chapter 1, then reassign it with lists. Most students can see the dramatic improvement in time achieved through lists for this problem;

7. Section 1 is very important. Binary trees are an important structure.
    This Morse Code program (exercise problem 1) is a good one to assign so
    that even students who are having difficulties can gain a little confi-
    dence. Sections 2 and 3 are the great separators. The two pointer rep-
    resentation of n-ary trees is a must. We prefer to assign a dictionary
    tree problem, like problem 9, to determine which students really under-
    stand the material. The three pointer representation of trees is not very
    important, but the tree searching in section 4 is;

8. In this chapter we normally emphasize the vector representation of di-
    graphs and briefly illustrate its relationship to a dynamically allocated
    linked record representation. Sections 1 through 3 are required. The
    purpose of section 4, on speeding up the vector or record representa-
    tions, must also be understood. Typically we briefly cover section 5 and
    give a programming problem related to one of the classical graph prob-
    lems. Section 6 is strictly optional and very difficult for many students.
    We recommend that it be assigned as optional, material for only the better
    students. It is the basis of VSAM or B*-tree file structures;

9. The first four sections contain standard material on sorting and should be
    covered completely. This includes material on tape sorting using a poly-
    phase merge sort. Section five is strictly optional;

10. The first two sections are basic material. Sections 3 and 4 go together in
    that address calculation sets a framework for hashing. Section 5 might
    be considered by some teachers to be optional. However, it does present
    two important features of the block sequential search:

    a. It is a natural compromise between the search and update timings of
        the sequential and bisection searches;

    b. It is the foundation from which ISAM files evolved;

11. Chapters 11 through 14 should all be considered optional to some extent,
    depending upon what the teacher wishes to emphasize. Many might argue
    that recursion should have been presented earlier. Perhaps, but by pre-
    senting it here we have an opportunity to go back over some areas, espe-
    cially trees and graphs, for a second time and give students a chance to
    take another look. This time, with the tool of recursion, some students
    might gain new insights;

12. This chapter presents a general overview of some of the techniques that
    have been employed to carry out dynamic storage allocation. This chap-
    ter is not intended to be comprehensive;

13. Take your pick. Sections 1 and 2 are fairly classical material. Section 3
    was suggested from a CAD/CAM problem. Section 4 is for game lovers.
    Section 5 is one of my favorites, namely, Hamming error correcting codes.
    It is a beautiful use of set theory;

14. The real challenge in data structures is mating the proper data structures with available hardware to solve real problems. Data base is one of these areas.

In general, the core of the text is chapters four through 10. The other material supports this core. Some might find the organization a bit unusual. Our concern was to introduce dynamic allocation early enough in the semester so that appropriate programming assignments could be presented early enough in the semester and that students have enough time to develop their solutions. We also felt that it was important to spiral through the material. That is, present topics several times in the text and give students time to digest material before we return to a topic in greater depth.

All the programs are formatted using the same scheme. Programs appear without any comments for several reasons. Our primary reason for doing this was so that all programs would appear either on a single page or on facing pages. We felt that it was educationally more sound for students to see the whole program without turning any pages so that they could visually observe the control structures in a program. All programs that are on two pages are broken at a logical point, typically before a procedure definition, so that they are easier to follow.

I would be remiss if I did not explicitly acknowledge some of the many people who directly or indirectly contributed to this text. Starting with my doctoral studies at Penn State, I was fortunate to meet many people who had a positive influence on me; Neil Jones, Raymond Yeh, Preston Hammer, Gene Singletary, Bruce Barnes, and Ben Honkanen, just to name a few. Also influential were Dick Austing (who evaluated our undergraduate computer science program in 1972) and Jerry Wagener. Jerry introduced me to the Morse Code Problem which is one of the best assignments you can use to introduce students to binary trees.

This text was set using Waterloo SCRIPT on an IBM 3033 with an attached Systems 6 laser printer at GTE Laboratories in Waltham, Mass. Dr. Paul Ritt, the Vice President of GTE Laboratories, and Dr. John Ambrose, Director of External Technical Affairs were instrumental in providing many opportunities for me to use their facilities at the Laboratories. They are to be commended for their continued interest in academic/government/industrial interaction through their recently established Academic Advisory Council.

Many of my colleagues at the University of Scranton provided much encouragement and support. A special thanks to my dean, Bill Parente, and some of our mathematics faculty, Ed Bartley, Gary Eichelsdorfer, Bernie Johns, and Ron Sinzdak, all of whom gave me considerable moral support although they were never really sure what I was doing.

John Meinke, Andrew Plonsky, and Chip Taylor were extremely helpful with their comments and suggestions. Andy provided me with a program to create the index for this text. Our students deserve a vote of thanks. They suffered through some early rough versions of this text. Many of them contributed directly with various types of assistance. These include Peggy Wagner, Linda Stercula, Greg Bohn, Mark Wisniewski, and Laura Antinori.

With regard to technical details of the layout, artwork, etc., Mike Meehan of Allyn and Bacon provided encouragement. He also provided three very critical reviewers. Fortunately I have a thick skin and incorporated a substantial number of the suggestions of the reviewers. I only hope that I have done them justice through my interpretations of their many suggestions.

Last but not least I must acknowledge two people who put some of the finishing touches on the text. Deborah Schneck did a beautiful job with the artwork. Her interpretations of my sketches were outstanding. Our friend Anne Lavelle proofread the text and removed many glaring typos and gramatical errors. If any still remain, I take the final responsibility for the mistakes. All those mentioned above, and many others, deserve the credit.

(Second printing) An advantage of a word processor is the opportunity to clean up your act, or at least improve upon it with some ease. Many observations were made about several errors in the first printing. In particular, I would like to thank Carmen Juinta, Mark Kerstetter and Thomas Mertz for their interest and helpful assistance.

John Beidler

1

Introduction
to Data Structures

The word "structure" has a meaning that should not have to be described. However, when asked to state the structure of a building, a college, or a corporation, different people give different answers depending upon their points of view. That is the basis of many programming problems, namely, obtaining the correct point of view in order to properly look at the structure of a problem and the structures that lead to an efficient solution. By structure in a program or in data, we mean both its real structure, how it actually exists in a computer, and its implied structure, how it is used.

The title, **Data Structures**, should not be misleading. The emphasis in data structures is the presentation of many different ways of representing information. However, these methods of organizing data are almost useless unless measurements are made of their costs, in time and space, relative to other techniques. It is important that all of the possible ramifications of the word "structure" are understood. Also, the goal is not "the ultimate data structure", but an understanding of "trade-offs." That is, when faced with several ways of representing or accessing information, typically, in gaining some advantage with one method, there is a corresponding cost, and choices must be made.

1:1. Logical Structure vs. Physical Structure

Within an object there may be many different structures. A building might be viewed by an architect as a particular organization of spaces of various dimensions. A structural engineer might view the same building as a collection of stresses on beams and other building materials. The owner of the building might view the structure of the building in terms of its functionality. Who is right? They are all correct because each description tells us something about the structure of the building, from different points of view. The architect views the building as an aesthetic structure, the engineer views it as the realization of a mathematical model of stresses, while the owner views it in terms of his ability to utilize the space.

Consider a specific example, a library. What is the structure of a library? Physically, it is a building filled mainly with shelves that contain books. There is also a logical structure in a library. It is the catalogue, index, or information retrieval system that locates the items in the library. These two views of a library are analogous to the problems encountered in computing. With a library, two questions continually arise. How can the physical space of the library be more fully utilized? What can be done to make it easier for people to access information in a library? The answers to these questions are reflected in changes that are made to the physical and logical structure in a library. New types of space allocation, microfilm, etc., influence the physical structure. New indexing schemes and retrieval methods influence the logical structure. Like a library, a computer has both physical and logical structures. The primary memory of a computer, regardless of the actual hardware that is being used, is a single large one dimensional array, regardless of how a programmer might think of using it when he programs. Logical structures are imposed on this one dimensional array through the ways that programs access memory. For example, suppose a programmer wishes to define a two dimensional array A [4,7]. Although the programmer can view a piece of memory as if it is a 4 by 7 two dimensional structure, this structure actually exists as 28 consecutive memory locations. The interface between the programmer's logical view and the actual allocation of the memory is carried out by the programming language. In FORTRAN, a two dimensional array is allocated a column at a time, see figure 1.1. When a program accesses an array, such as,

$$A (K,J),$$

it uses K and J to compute a single index,

$$4*(J-1) + K$$

as the index into the one dimensional equivalent to the two dimensional array.

This is a data structure. It allows a programmer to design algorithms which use two dimensional arrays without having to concern himself with the details of array representation. This means that the programmer can concentrate his efforts on solving his problem. This is the positive side of this tradeoff, but what is the cost? In the case of a two dimensional array, the cost is minimal in that the computer automatically carries out the necessary calculations the programmer would have had to make to access the structure. The cost to carry out this data structure is only the time it takes to calculate the index

$$4*(J-1)+K.$$

Suppose a compiler did not support two dimensional arrays. They really are not necessary because, from above, they can be simulated in a one dimensional array. That may be true, but what problems would occur if two dimensional structures were not available to programmers? What kinds of programming errors would be made? Although there might be some cost in data structures, there is always the possibility of the immeasurable benefit of improved programmer performance. This is because, having the two dimensional array available to a programmer means that the compiler handles the implementational details and the programmer can concentrate on what the program is doing rather than how it is carrying it out. An important part of data structures is separating the physical details of how certain things are carried out from the logical requirements of what is supposed to be accomplished.

1:2. Some Data Structures

Data Structures is the study of methods of interfacing the ways programmers view the data and the interrelations between information with the realities of the devices, especially computer memories, which store the information. Data structures are actually a combination of methods of organizing information and algorithms to efficiently access and manipulate data. Therefore, our interest is not just in cataloging storage techniques and algorithms. It is vitally important to measure the costs of various storage techniques as well as the appropriateness of their use in various situations.

The primary memory of any computing system can be thought of as a one dimensional array. Some basic data structures are already given to us by most programming language compilers, for example, two and three dimensional arrays. In section 1:1, the columnwise representation of a two dimensional array in a one dimensional array was described. Suppose a rowwise organization was desirable. Let A be a two dimensional array, M by N. In a rowwise organization, each of the M rows contains N locations. The third part of figure 1.1 illustrates the rowwise allocation of a 4 by 7 array. For rowwise allocation of an M by N array, the position A [K,J] in an array is accessed with the index calculation

$$N*(K-1)+J \ .$$

Higher dimensioned structures can be stored in one dimensional arrays and accessed by the construction of various index calculation formulas. The ideas of rowwise and columnwise allocation can be generalized to other dimensions. For example, a three dimensional array can be allocated in several ways. Let B be an M1 by M2 by M3 three dimensional array. It can be allocated one dimension at a time. The equivalent to columnwise allocation is to allocate one dimension at a time, starting with the first dimension. That is B [1,1,1] occupies the first position in the array, B [2,1,1] occupies the second, etc., then B [1,2,1] is allocated immediately after B [M1,1,1]. This is accomplished through the indexing formula The position B [J, K, L] is accessed through the indexing formula

$$M1*M2*(L-1) \ + \ M1*(K-1) \ + \ J \ .$$

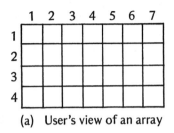

(a)   User's view of an array

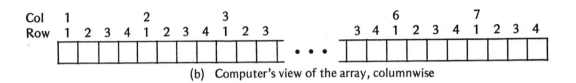

(b)   Computer's view of the array, columnwise

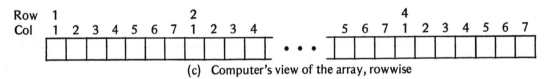

(c)   Computer's view of the array, rowwise

Figure 1.1.   Logical and physical views of matrix allocation

To see this, one less than L, L-1, is the number of M1 by M2 levels of the three dimensional array that must precede any given level.   One less than K, K-1, is the number of columns of size M1 that must precede a given row in this level, and J is the position of this item in this column.

Various formulas can be obtained depending upon the order in which the dimensions are allocated.   Also, the formulas can be directly generalized to any number of dimensions.

A **matrix** is a two dimensional array of values where both dimensions are fixed.   A **square matrix** is a matrix where the number of rows equals the number of columns.   A data structure which is not usually implemented by compilers is the **triangular matrix** as shown in figure 1.2.   Figure 1.2 illustrates an order 4 lower triangular matrix.   A **lower triangular matrix** is a two dimensional data structure where position (i,j) exists only if i ≥ j.   An upper triangular matrix is a triangular matrix where position (i,j) exists only if i ≤ j.   The formula for determining the index for rowwise allocation of a lower triangular matrix uses the observation that row i contains i locations, therefore the index to position (i,j) is

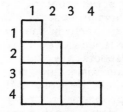

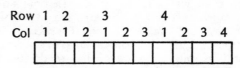

(a) User's view of a triangular matrix   (b) Computer's view of a triangular matrix

Figure 1.2. **Lower triangular matrix, row-wise allocation**

$$1 + 2 + ... + (i-1) + j .$$

The formula for the sum of the first n digits is

$$1 + 2 + ... + n = n(n+1)/2$$

which simplifies the index formula to

$$j + (i-1)*i/2 .$$

Columnwise allocation of lower triangular matrices as well as allocation formulas for rowwise and columnwise allocation of upper triangular matrices are given as exercises.

1:3. Trade Offs

There are many considerations that must be made when writing programs. Not all of these considerations are quantitative. For example, how readable is a program? It is important to remember that programs must be read by humans as well as by computers. In fact, the biggest problems faced in software development is the modification of programs. How can a human programmer modify a program that cannot be read? The most sophisticated program can be almost worthless if it is not documented in such a way that others can read and understand how the program functions. Occasionally, a programmer learning new data structure methods gets carried away. What good is a cute program filled with clever techniques if it is only going to be used once or twice and it takes three weeks to write and debug the program when the whole operation could be done manually in one day? Obviously, the answer is - it does no good at all. This is why measurement is so important.

By understanding the costs of an approach, it can be measured against other alternatives and the relative merits of an approach can be determined.

One consideration which programmers must take into account as a program is being designed and implemented is the programmer's personal resources. The programmer's resources are the human time and human space (paper, black-boards, tables, file cabinets, rooms, etc.) used to perform the programming process as well as the computer time and computer space used to encode, de-bug, and carry out the program. The human aspects are very difficult to measure, but must be considered. The computer time and space can be measured, but even these measurements can sometimes be very difficult. Al-ternatives must be carefully evaluated while a program is being designed. Specifically, decisions about space allocations can affect the program's execu-tion time, and vice versa.

```
1   PROGRAM indexsort ( input, output );
2
3   TYPE
4       intarray = ARRAY [ 1..1000 ] OF integer;
5
6   PROCEDURE
7       indexsort ( data:  intarray;
8                   VAR index: intarray;
9                   size: integer );
10
11      VAR
12          i, j, extra: integer;
13
14      BEGIN
15      FOR i := 1 TO size DO
16          index [i] := i;
17      FOR i := 1 TO size-1 DO
18          BEGIN
19          j := i;
20          WHILE (j > 0) AND (data [index [j] ] > data [index [j+1]. DO
21              BEGIN
22              extra := index [j];  index [j] := index [j+1];
23              index [j+1] := extra;   j := j-1
24              END
25          END
26      END;
27
28  BEGIN
29  END.
```

Figure 1.3. A Sort Using Pointers

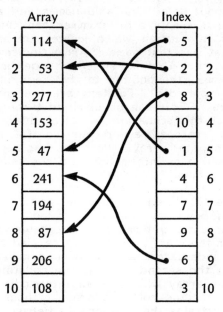

Figure 1.4.   Illustration of the results of a logical sort

Fortunately, time-space trade-off considerations have little effect on most human interaction considerations. Speed and program efficiency should not be used as excuses for writing programs that are unreadable or cannot be maintained. However, one good measure of a well written program is this: A program by its very existence changes its environment. It can provide new information which in turn suggests further enhancements to the program. If a program can be easily modified so that it can be changed to keep abreast of its changing environment is one of the best tests of the quality of the original design of the program.

As data structure techniques are attempted, the importance of good programming practices becomes more apparent. In particular, by carefully studying the logical requirements of a problem, and working out the logical requirements before generating code, many potential difficulties will be bypassed. If more time is spent understanding a problem and designing the logical requirements of an algorithm, then less time will be spent patching and debugging an inappropriate program.

1:4. Pointers

A key concept in data structures is the generalization of the concept of an index, called a **pointer**. A **pointer** is a variable in a program that contains location information about data. Variable names and array indices are pointers. A variable name is simply a programmer convenience interpreted by the compiler into address information which locates the memory location used to hold the data item that has that name. Array indices are also pointers, but they are **relative pointers**. That is, an array index must be used in conjunction with an array name (the pointer to the beginning of the array). But why emphasize this simple idea? Pointers are the root of the implementation of many data structures. This can be clarified through an example of a sorting problem. Consider this scenario: A set of numbers in an array is to be sorted, however, for reasons beyond our control the numbers cannot be moved or copied into another array. Perhaps it is because each number associates to a large collection of information and the collection would have to be moved along with the number.

The program in figure 1.3 illustrates how the sort can be carried out logically by using an array of pointers, the array called INDEX. The array INDEX does not contain basic data, but rather, it contains information about the location of data. After this sort procedure is carried out, INDEX [1] contains the relative pointer, index, to the first item in collating order. INDEX [2] contains the index to the second item in the collating order, and so forth. In this way, using the array INDEX as an intermediary, the items in ARRAY can be accessed in ascending collating order without moving the actual data items. Figure 1.4 illustrates the relationship between INDEX and ARRAY for an array of 10 values. The 5 in INDEX [1] points to the smallest number in ARRAY which is in the fifth location. Figure 1.4 illustrates the results of the procedure in figure 1.3 for an array of 10 values.

The procedure in figure 1.5 prints the values in DATA using the array INDEX so that the numbers are printed in collating order. That is, as a result of INDEXSORT, the procedure INDEXPRINT uses INDEX [1] to access the first number,

DATA [INDEX [1]] .

Similarly, using INDEX [2] the second value is accessed, and so forth. The outer loop in figure 1.5 is used to count the number of values printed on each line.

The procedure INDEXSORT in figure 1.3 is a typical bubble sort procedure but with a slight twist. In a normal bubble sort, as shown in figure 1.6, the array INDEX would not be used. In particular, compare lines 20 through 23 of figure 1.3 with lines 17 through 20 of figure 1.6. In the bubble sort (figure 1.6), two adjacent values in DATA are compared, then interchanged if not in the right order. If two numbers are interchanged, then the inner loop continues to execute and bubble a value up in the array DATA until it is

```
1   PROGRAM indexprint ( input, output );
2
3   TYPE
4       intarray = ARRAY [ 1..1000 ] OF integer;
5
6   PROCEDURE
7       indexprint ( data :  intarray;
8                      VAR index : intarray;
9                      size : integer );
10
11      VAR
12          i, j : integer;
13
14      BEGIN
15      i := 1;
16      WHILE i <= size DO
17          BEGIN
18          j := 0;
19          WHILE (i <= size) AND ( j < 10 ) DO
20              BEGIN
21              write( data [index [i] ]:10 );
22              i := i+1;   j := j+1
23              END;
24          writeln
25          END
26      END;
27
28  BEGIN
29  END.
```

Figure 1.5.   Procedure to print an ordered list of logically sorted values

placed in proper collating order.   In the program of figure 1.3, the values in DATA are never moved.   Rather, the numbers in INDEX are moved so that INDEX [1] points to the first number in DATA, INDEX [2] points to the second, etc.   By using the array INDEX, the sort in figure 1.3 "logically" accomplished the same result that is "physically" carried out in figure 1.6.

1:5. EXERCISES

1. Rowwise and columnwise allocation of matrices have analogies to allocation of multi-dimensional arrays.   Allocating an array starting with the first dimension is analogous to rowwise allocation.

    a. For a three dimensional array, A, with dimensions M, N, and O, find the formula that determines the index into the one dimensional equivalent when one accesses A [J,K,L] assuming rowwise allocation.

```
 1   PROGRAM bubblesort ( input, output );
 2
 3   TYPE
 4        intarray = ARRAY [ 1..1000 ] OF integer;
 5
 6   PROCEDURE
 7        bubble ( data :   intarray;
 8                  size : integer );
 9
10       VAR
11            i, j, extra: integer;
12
13       BEGIN
14       FOR i := 1 TO size-1 DO
15            BEGIN
16            j := i;
17            WHILE (j > 0) AND (data [j]   > data [j+1] ) DO
18                 BEGIN
19                 extra := data [j];   data [j] := data [j+1];
20                 data [j+1] := extra;   j := j-1
21                 END
22            END
23        END;
24
25   BEGIN
26   END.
```

Figure 1.6.   A typical bubble sort procedure

    b.   Do the same for columnwise allocation.
    c.   Determine rowwise and columnwise index formulas for n dimensional
        arrays.

2.   Determine the index formula for rowwise allocation of a four dimensional
    array.   Do the same for columnwise allocation.

3.   Determine the allocation formula for columnwise allocation of a lower trian-
    gular matrix.

4.   What relationships exist between the formulas for rowwise and columnwise
    allocation of lower and upper triangular matrices?

5.   Write routines to allocate a Pascal triangle as shown below as a lower tri-
    angular matrix using rowwise allocation.   Do the same using columnwise
    allocation. Which is more appropriate?   Why?   Write routines to appropri-
    ately print the matrix.

Figure 1.7. A Pascal Triangle of order 5

6. Figure 1.3 illustrates a program which sets up an array of pointers so that numbers can be accessed in ascending collating order. Write a routine

    LNKSRT(ARRAY,LINK,SIZE,FIRST)

    in which ARRAY,LINK, and SIZE are as in figure 1.3 except that FIRST contains the index to the smallest number in collating order and LINK [J] contains the index to the next number in order following ARRAY [J]. If the last number in collating order is ARRAY [J], then LINK [J] = 0. Figure 1.8 illustrates the contents of tne locations for the same values as in the array 1.4. Note how the contents of LINK [J] point to the next item in order after the value in ARRAY [J].

7. A word search is a matrix of letters. There are words in the matrix, the words can be spelled horizontally, vertically, or diagonally, left-to-right, or right-to-left. Write a program to set up a word search in a matrix, then read in words one at a time and find them in the matrix. Determine the maximum number of loop iterations that would be required to find a word in an m by n matrix if the word is of size s. Figure 1.9 illustrates a word search matrix and a set of words that appear in the matrix.

8. An interesting game is Conway's solitaire game called life. The game is played on a matrix. Randomly place several x's at various positions on a matrix. Those x's represent a generation of curious little creatures that have strange rules for birth, death, and procreation as life continues from one generation to the next on the matrix. The eight positions surrounding each position are called neighbors of that position. The rules for establishment of the next generation are as follows:

    1. Any creature with more than three neighbors dies of overpopulation;
    2. Any creature with fewer than two neighbors dies of loneliness;
    3. Birth occurs on any vacant location with exactly three neighbors.

Write a program which flips back and forth between two matrices to create each generation of some starting pattern of life. For example, if generation 1 appears in matrix A, then generation 2 appears in matrix B. Then using matrix B, create generation 3 in matrix A, and so forth. Determine the maxi-

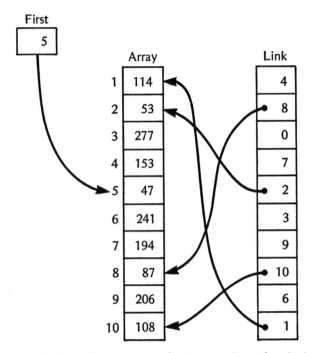

Figure 1.8.   Illustration of the results of a linked sort

mum number of loop iterations required by the program to obtain one generation from the previous generation.

```
ACHONEROX-CP-VSBP
OBOOPYECRUOSLDIIZ
DXNOKBOFULPAOKRMR
HWEEERTKMCYOIEPAT
GOYREKNEOPOVJMDBC
ARWUOIMORXAKKCOBS
LYENLXESYMBIONTEI
FILEMOSEGXIPSMRSD
OKLCNPBIJDYNEOPIE
REAPSASOGHRTASUBM
TPLUSXLICMYONLNMO
RZAIOAITIBAOWIC1I
ATCRYXAIRLBVTEH8B
NCELLBURROUGHS205
KXTSILOGLASSIGNOX
```

ALGOL	COPY	PUNCH
APL	CORE	RAD
ASSIGN	CPU	ROM
BASIC	DISC	RUN
BATCH	FILE	SNOBOL
BIOMED	FORTRAN	SORT
BIT	HONEYWELL	SOURCE
BPM	IBM1800	SPSS
BTM	KEY	SYMBIONT
BURROUGHS205	LINK	TAPE
BYTE	LIST	TERMINAL
CARD	LMN	TREE
CELL	OLAY	WORD
COBOL	PCL	

Figure 1.9.   A word search problem

2

Program Measurement

Structured programming helps programmers make more effective use of their time. But once a program exists, new questions arise. In particular, how well does a program use its resources? What are the program's time and space requirements? Does the program make efficient use of its resources? Which variables influence the programs resources? What effects do these variables have on the resources? Structured programming helps us answer some of these questions.

Basically, given a computer system, a program has two resources, time and space, whose usage is influenced by three factors - the hardware, the algorithm, and the data. What are the typical effects these factors have on the time and space requirements of a program? Hardware, algorithm, and data all influence the timing. But hardware considerations depend quite heavily upon the particular hardware/software configuration being used. Therefore, after taking a brief look at the role of hardware, this section concentrates on ways of measuring the effects of the algorithm and the data on the program's timing. Basic techniques of measuring a program's time requirement and methods of recognizing certain recurring timing situations are described. Similar techniques can be used to obtain space requirements for programs.

There is no complete and exhaustive collection of program measurement techniques. Program measurement can be difficult, tedious, and sometimes impossible. Therefore, in this chapter only a few basic methods are presented. These simple measurement techniques help us measure the time and space requirements of a large collection of programs. These techniques are expanded on throughout the text.

2:1. Space and Time Measurement

While a program is being developed, there should always be a concern for the amount of time and space that the program will require. **Space requirement** means the amount of memory and peripheral storage used by a program. For a program, the space requirement is the sum of the space for the program and the data space. Each of these space requirements can be broken down further into the amount of primary (main memory) and secondary (disk, tape, etc.) storage that is needed. By **program space** we mean the actual space in memory that contains the program. Program space is very dependent upon the hardware/software configuration of each computing system. For example, if a compiler is used, the space requirements for the program are considerably different than if an interpreter is used. Instruction repertoire, addressing methods, operating systems conventions, etc., all play a role in the size of a program. Specifics of a particular computing system play an important role in a program's space requirements. Normally, a programmer must write a program to function in a given hardware/software environment. Also, once a program is executing the program does not change. Therefore, there are very few general principles that can be developed regarding the measurement of the space requirements for the program.

Data space also depends upon hardware. However there are some general observations that can be made about the amount of data space required by a program and how the size of the data space depends upon an algorithm and a program's input. The techniques that are used to arrive at estimates of data storage requirements are similar to the techniques that are used to measure time requirements. Also, typically, time measurements produce a richer collection of functional relationships and the time requirements of a program can be affected by the space available to a program. As a matter of fact, a key issue in programming is the trade-off that can exist between time and space measurements. That is, changing the space available to a program can adversely affect the timing and taking advantage of additional space can speed up a program.

A further consideration about data storage requirements is the peripheral space needed to store very large collections of data. This is very important in the study of data base systems. Since data bases are beyond the scope of this text and because of the dependence of storage requirements on the particulars of specific storage devices, this subject is not emphasized here.

Time requirement means the amount of time used by a program. Time requirements can be thought of in several different ways, the amount of central processor time, the amount of "wall time" (that is, the actual time from the start to the end of a program), I/O time, etc. The amount of time and space required by a program directly depend upon:

1. The actual hardware
2. The algorithmic structure of the program
3. The data processed by the program

The type of computer hardware used can affect both the time and space requirements of a program. The speed of the hardware, the configuration of the memory, the memory addressing and many other hardware related items affect a program's efficiency. Since the measure of the effect of hardware on an algorithm relates directly to the particular equipment being used, this measurement can be tedious, difficult, and extremely dependent upon the computer system being used. However, the effect of hardware relative to the effects of the structure of an algorithm or of the data can be observed without getting into details about hardware. This is described in an example below. In order to avoid some potential timing difficulties, several assumptions are made about the timing of basic program steps regardless of the hardware. These assumptions are not always true, however, when the assumptions fail the actual timing is less than or equal to the timing obtained here.

With regard to the structure of algorithms, there are four considerations, the three basic control constructs and modularization, specifically:

1. Sequencing of program steps
2. Loop control
3. Conditional code execution
4. Modularization

With regard to sequences of code, the total time for a sequence of code is the sum of the timings for the individual steps in the sequence. To see this, consider any two consecutive elementary program statements in the program in figure 2.1, for example, lines 19 and 20. The total time to execute two of these steps is the sum total of the execution time of these two steps, unless there are special hardware considerations that must be taken into account. For example, there are computers whose hardware will execute some statement sequences faster than others although the statement sequences perform identical operations. For these types of hardware situations, the timing results obtained here are greater than or equal to the actual results.

For loops (figure 2.1, lines 12 through 16), the timing depends upon the number of times the loop iterates as well as the hardware time for the instructions in the loop and the hardware time for the loop decision. If a loop performs N times, the time to perform the instructions within a loop is L, and the time for one execution of the loop decision is D, the total loop execution time is

$$N*L + (N+1)*D = N*(L+D) + D.$$

N does not depend on the hardware but on the algorithm and the data values. N might possibly be a function of one or more variables. Note that the decision on line 35 in the program performs N+1 times when the loop executes N times.

The execution of an IF structure (for example lines 8 through 16 in figure 2.1) can be broken down as follows: Let D be the hardware time for the decision, B1 the time for the block of code that performs if the decision is true, and B2 the execute time for the block of code if the decision is false. When an IF structure performs, the decision always executes, then either block, but not both, execute. Therefore, the time for a conditional structure is

$$D+B1 \text{ or } D+B2$$

```
1 PROGRAM revolvingcharge (input, output);
2
3 VAR
4     month: integer;
5     rate, amount, balance, payment, totalint, int: real;
6
7 PROCEDURE
8     monthly;
9
10     BEGIN
11     int := balance * rate;   totalint := totalint + int;
12     month := month + 1;
13     write(month:5,amount:15:2);
14     IF payment >= (amount + int) THEN
15         BEGIN
16         payment := amount + int;   balance := 0.0
17         END
18     ELSE
19         balance := amount + int - payment;
20     amount := balance;
21     writeln(int:7:2,balance:15:2,totalint:10:2)
22     END;
23
24 BEGIN  { program }
25 reset(input);   read(amount, rate, payment); balance := 0.0;
26 write(' LOAN PAYMENT SCHEDULE FOR A LOAN OF',amount:12:2);
27 write('  PAID AT THE RATE OF',payment:7:2,' PER MONTH AT ');
28 writeln(rate:7:4);
29 write(' MONTH','BALANCE ':15,'INTEREST','NEW BALANCE':14);
30 writeln('TOT. PAID');
31 rate := rate / 12.0 / 100.0;   month := 0;   totalint := 0;
32 IF payment <= amount * rate THEN
33         writeln('B**** PAYMENT TOO SMALL ****',payment:10:2)
34     ELSE
35         WHILE amount > 0.0 DO
36         monthly
37 END.
```

Figure 2.1. A loan payment program

but not both.

Because, as you will see below, program timing can produce very complex equations, simply obtaining bounds on the execution time is important. Consequently, depending upon the time bound being sought, upper or lower, the execution time for a conditional structure is bound below by

$$D + MIN(B1, B2)$$

and bound above by

$$D + MAX(B1, B2)$$

where MIN and MAX are functions whose values are equal to the smallest and the largest values of their arguments, respectively.

Next, consider the effect on timing due to modularization (line 13, figure 2.1). If a module is called from a particular position in a program, the effect on the program's time relative to that particular call is M, where M is the execute time of that module. There is some hardware consideration that should be made relative to modularization. Depending upon the techniques employed by various computer systems, the cost of performing a module of code is slightly more than if the code were in the position where the reference was made. Rather than being concerned at this point with that time requirement, assume that M includes that hardware overhead or is negligible.

Before looking at the effect the actual data values have on a program, let us consider an example to illustrate how timings go together. Figure 2.1 is a program which produces a month by month summary of the status of a consumer loan. In order to determine the execution time of this program, the following notation is used:

1. S - Sequence of basic instructions
2. L - A loop structure
3. I - An IF structure
4. B - A remote block or subprogram
5. C - The expression that controls a condition or block execution.

In order to reference the location in a program, these notations are used in conjunction with location information. For example,

$$S_{3-9}$$

signifies the time required to perform the sequence of basic statements 3 through 9.

Using this notation and the structure of the program in figure 2.1 the initial evaluation of the execute time, T, of the program is

$$T = S_{24-31} + I_{32-36} + S_{37}.$$

I_{32-36} can be further described as satisfying

$$I_{32-36} \leq C_{32} + MAX(S_{33}, S_{34} + L_{35-36}).$$

The loop time $L_{35\text{-}36}$ satisfies

$$L_{35\text{-}36} = N_{35}*(\ C_{35}\ +\ B_{36}\ )\ +\ C_{35}$$

where N_{35} is the number of iterations of the loop. The block, B_{36}, execution is bound by

$$B_{36} \leq S_{10\text{-}13}\ +\ C_{\ 14}\ +\ MAX(S_{15\text{-}17},S_{19}\ )\ +\ S_{20\text{-}22}.$$

Combining all of this produces the time bound

$$T \leq S_{24\text{-}31}\ +\ C_{32}$$

$$MAX(S_{33},S_{34}\ +\ N_{35}\ *(\ C_{35}\ +\ S_{10\text{-}13}\ +\ C_{14}$$

$$MAX(S_{15\text{-}17},S_{19})\ +\ S_{20\text{-}22})+\ C_{35})+\ S_{37}.$$

Observe that just a simple program can create a complex timing equation. In order to get a better grasp of the relative impacts of hardware and algorithm on timing, and since at this point only an upper bound on the timing would be sufficient, let K be a constant amount of time such that K is greater than or equal to the amount of time required to carry out any basic sequences of instructions in the program, including the execution of conditional expressions. Then the relation that bounds T becomes

$$T \leq K\ +\ K\ +\ MAX(\ K,K\ +\ N_{35}\ *$$

$$(\ K\ +\ K\ +\ K\ +\ MAX(\ K,K\ )\ +\ K\ )\ +\ K\ )\ +\ K,$$

which simplifies to

$$T \leq 3K\ +\ MAX(\ K,2K\ +\ N_{35}*5K) \leq 5K\ +\ 5K*N_{35} = K(5+5N_{35}\ ).$$

This example illustrates several observations that are generally true about timing equations. First, to simplify timing expressions, find a constant K which bounds the execution time of all elementary sequences of instructions in the program. This can be difficult to do for each particular system and program, but it can be assumed that such a bound exists. Second, in the timing expression, replace all elementary timing sequences by K and simplify the expression. Third, whenever possible, simplify all MAX functions by replacing them by the maximum value, if it can be determined.

At this point, the resulting inequality,

$$T \leq K*(5\ +\ 5\ N_{35}\ ),$$

indicates the typical effect of hardware on computer timing. Actually, it can be extracted from the equation and placed as a constant multiple at the front of the expression. This can be an important consideration. The difference between K equals .5 millisecond and K equals 2 milliseconds could mean the difference between 15 minutes and one hour, a factor of four.

Hardware does have an effect on program execution time, but the remainder of the equation depends upon the algorithm and the data manipulated by the program. Normally a programmer has little control over the available hardware. Generally, the form of the equation depends upon the algorithm and the remaining variables. For example, N_{35}, depends upon the data. The interaction between the structure of the algorithm and the amount and organization of the data leads directly to the heart of trade-off problems and decisions that must be made while a program is being designed.

The data being processed by a program can affect the time and space requirements of the program. Here, three items must be considered:

1. The amount of data
2. The actual values of the data items
3. The organization of the data

Obviously the amount of data affects a program's time at least linearly. That is, processing more data takes more time just to read the data. The actual values themselves can affect the time of a program. For example, the program in figure 2.1 reads a set of data which represents the amount of a loan, the annual interest rate, and the monthly payments, then prints a monthly breakdown of the status of the loan. Obviously, the number of loop iterations performed by this program depends upon the relative values of these three items, and the number of loop iterations has a direct effect on the timing of the program. In the case of figure 2.1, finding the value of N_{14}, the number of loop iterations, requires some effort. The answer in this case is

$$N_{14} = INT(\frac{1}{r} LN(m/(m-y*r)))$$

where INT is the greatest integer function, LN is the natural logarithm function, and y, 100r, and m are the original values read into AMOUNT, RATE, and PAYMENT, respectively. The order of the data can also have an effect. The bubble sort illustrated in figure 2.2 demonstrates this. Assume that the numbers in the array passed to the bubble sort procedure are already in sorted order. Then the condition for exiting the inner loop is always satisfied, therefore, the inner loop does not execute. For any other possible arrangement of the data in the array, the inner loop would execute, therefore, the order of the data can have a very definite effect on the execution time of a program.

Obviously, the location (memory, disk, tape) of the data can also have an effect on program timing. However, the location is a hardware dependent consideration and will not be considered as a function of the data itself.

2:2. Timing Fundamentals

There is no simple set of rules that can guarantee that the time requirements of a program can always be determined. However, there are some basic mathematical skills that seem to help time and again. Trying to find the precise time can require knowledge about the problem at hand. For example, determining the timing equation for the problem in figure 2.1 demands knowledge about the equations that govern a loan payment, which can be solved through the use of finite difference equations or differential equations. Fortunately, there are many problems that can be solved with simpler mathematical techniques.

Very often, one simply wishes to find a bound on the program execution time or find the most important variable in the timing equation and concentrate on how the time changes as that variable gets larger. Specifically, if the time is a function of some variable n, say $T = f(n)$, we are interested in the growth of T as n becomes infinite. In order to simplify timing equations, we adopt the "big O" notation. We write

$$g(x) = O(f(x))$$

to mean there exist K and N such that

$$0 < g(x) < kf(x) \text{ whenever } x > N.$$

For example, suppose we have the timing equation,

$$T = 4n^4 + 23n^3 + 7n + 4.$$

As n becomes large, the dominant term in the timing equation is the fourth degree term. We can find K and N ($K = 6$, $N = 23$) such that

$$4n^4 + 23n^3 + 7n + 4 < 6n^4$$

whenever $n > 23$ and therefore

$$T = O(n^4).$$

This notation concentrates on the dominant terms in an equation. However, sometimes the big O notation removes too much. For example, in the timing obtained for the program in figure 2.1,

$$T = K(5 + 6N_{35}).$$

Technically, the result could be

$$T = O (N_{35}),$$

that is, the time is dominated by the number of loop iterations. But the 5 and 6 evolved from the algorithm and K depend upon the hardware. The big O notation is always used here to remove the hardware part of the timing, which is always a constant multiple. Depending upon other considerations, other constants and lower ordered terms might be kept. For the timing of figure 2.1 depending upon the emphasis,

$$O(5{+}6N_{35}), \quad O(6N_{35}), \quad \text{or } O(N_{35}).$$

could be written.

```
 1 PROGRAM indexsort ( input, output );
 2
 3 TYPE
 4     intarray = ARRAY [ 1..1000 ] OF integer;
 5
 6 PROCEDURE
 7     bubblesort ( VAR data:  intarray;
 8                  size: integer );
 9
10     VAR
11         i, j, extra: integer;
12
13     BEGIN
14     FOR i := 1 TO size-1 DO
15         BEGIN
16         j := i;
17         WHILE ( j > 0 ) AND ( data [j] > data [j+1] ) DO
18             BEGIN
19             extra := data [j];  data [j] := data [j+1];
20             data [j+1] := extra;   j := j-1
21             END
22         END
23     END;
```

Figure 2.2. Nested Loop Example - A Bubble Sort

Loop iterations dominate the timing functions for programs. Since this is the case, the key to many timing problems is determining the number of iterations of nested loops. To see this, consider the program in figure 2.2. Using the structure of the program and assuming that any sequence of instructions is bound by some constant K, the timing result is

$$T = 3K + L_{14-22} + K.$$

The loop, L_{14-22} is expanded as

$$L_{14-22} = K + N_{14}*(3K + L_{17-21}),$$

and the loop, L_{17-21} is expanded as

$$L_{17-21} = K + N_{17}*5K.$$

Putting this together and reducing yields

$$T = O(4*N_{14} + 5*N_{14} * N_{17}).$$

Now the problem is determining the functions and variables that replace the notation N_4 and N_6.

No simple set of rules tells how to do this, however, there are certain techniques which frequently solve this problem. These techniques are a collection of counting methods from:

1.   Combinatorics
2.   Graphical techniques
3.   Series summation
4.   Calculus
5.   Statistics

The following sections introduce the last four methods.

2:3. Timing Techniques - Graphing

It is not difficult to see that counting the number of loop iterations is the key to program timing. As you would suspect, this problem is compounded by nested loops. However, since structured programming eliminates overlapping loop structures, the problem is not as complicated as it could be. The key to timing nested loop structures is to carefully time each loop in the nested structure.

Consider the nested loop structure in figure 2.3. Three loops must be timed. The outer loop executes 10 times, but each time it executes, the number of iterations of the other two loops depend upon the value in i. The inner most loop, the K loop, depends upon the values of both i and j. One method of determining the number of iterations of each loop is to create a graphical representation of the number of loop iterations. With this method, each 1x1 square on a Cartesian plane represents one unit of time (see figure 2.4). This approach relates the coordinate axes to variables that control loop timing. To illustrate, consider the problem of timing the middle loop in figure

```
FOR i = 1 TO 10
    FOR j = i TO 10
        FOR k = i TO j

        { end of k loop }
    { end of j loop }
{ end of i loop }
```

Figure 2.3.   Sample nested loop

2.3, the j loop.   The number of iterations of the j loop depends upon the value of i.   Since i varies from 1 to 10, use the x-axis to represent the values of i, then use the squares in the interval between i-1 and i to count the number of loop iterations of the j loop within a single iteration of the variable i.   When i is 1, the j loop iterates 10 times, when i is 2, the j loop iterates 9 times, etc. .   As a result, figure 2.4 would represent a count of the total number of loop iterations of the j loop, which is 55.

Since the j loop iterates 55 times, the x-axis of a new graph is used to represent the 55 times the j loop iterates.   Then for each iteration of the j loop, the values of i and j are known and the number of iterations of the k loop is i-j+1.   The result is given in the graph in figure 2.5.

At this point two observations can be made about the graphics approach. First, counting the number of squares blocked off can become a challenge. Second, although it can be difficult to count the number of squares, the graph does indicate a pattern, for example, the "saw tooth" curve in figure 2.5.   The graphics approach organizes the counting of the loop iterations and pictorially represents the timing.   Now additional tools are required to count the number of squares that are blocked off.

2:4. Timing Techniques - Series Summation and Calculus

The results of a graphic representation of the timing of a program can normally be simplified through the use of series summation formulas.   One such formula is the summation formula for consecutive integers,

$$1 + 2 + \ldots + n = (n^2 + n)/2 \, .$$

Each saw tooth of the graph in figure 2.5 bounds an area equal to the sum of consecutive integers.   The first tooth bounds an area equal to the sum of the digits from 1 to 10, which equals 55, the second area equals 45 (the sum from 1 to 9), the third 36, etc. .   Adding these results together yields

$$55 + 45 + 36 + 28 + 21 + 15 + 10 + 6 + 3 + 1 = 220 \, .$$

Table 2.6 states several standard series summation formulas.

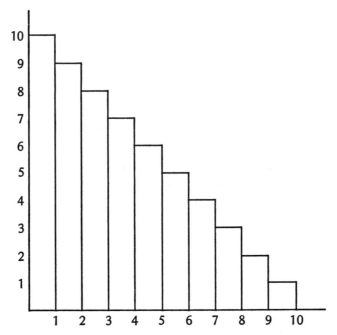

Figure 2.4. Graphical Representation of the number of loop iterations

Often, the loop iterations do not depend upon fixed values but on variables. For example, suppose the i loop in figure 2.3 was

FOR i = min TO max.

Now the number of iterations of the i loop is MAX-MIN+1, assuming Max >= MIN, otherwise the i loop does not execute. Then the number of iterations for the j loop also depends upon the values in MIN and MAX. In addition, the timing of the k loop appears to become more complex. However, by using the series summation formulas and the dominance (big O) notation the timing equation is reasonable. The second column in table 2.6 shows the dominance relations in the summation formulas. That is, as the timing formula gets more complicated, the dominant term is the most important part of the equation.

Another way to approach this is to use calculus, specifically, integration. Remember, timing functions can quickly become very complex, therefore some-times it is sufficient to simply obtain the order of magnitude of the timing function. The graphical approach associates the timing of a function to an

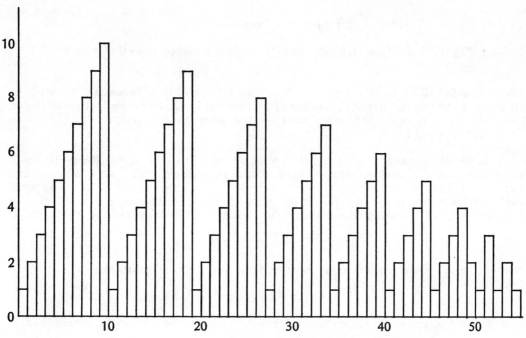

Figure 2.5. Timing for the "K" loop in figure 2.3

$$1 + 2 + \ldots + n = (n^2 + n)/2$$

$$1^2 + 2^2 + 3^2 + \cdots + n^2 = n(n+1)(2n+1)/6$$

$$1^k + 2^k + 3^k + \cdots + n^k = O(n^{k+1}/(k+1))$$

Table 2.6. Some Series Summation Formulas.

area in a Cartesian plane. Find a function which bounds that area, in that the area between the function and the x-axis is approximately equal to the area associated to the program time. For example, consider the area in figure 2.4. The function, y = 11-x bounds an area which contains the area equal to the timing of the loop. Area under a curve is found through integration and the integral of 11-x from x=0 to x=10 is greater than the time of the loop. Also, the function y = 10-x could have been used. Here, the area

```
FOR i = 1 TO n
   For j = 1 to i

   { end of j loop }

   { end of i loop }
```

Figure 2.7. Nested loop example with variable iteration count

under the function is slightly less than the timing area. However, as long as only an estimate is needed, either function will do because both functions have the same growth characteristics as the area on the graph which defines the program's time.

This becomes more apparent if the number of loop iterations depends upon some variable. Consider the nested loops in figure 2.7. A graph of the number of loop iterations of the inner loop appears in figure 2.8. The area that represents the timing is closely bound by the function $y = x$ or the function $y = x+1$. Integrating these functions from 0 to n yield the results

$$n^2/2 \text{ and } n^2/2 + n$$

respectively. Both answers are of the same order of magnitude,

$$O(n^2) = O(n^2/2) = O(n^2/2 + n),$$

and hence the order of magnitude of the growth of the timing is determined.

2:5. Getting a Handle on Timing

The number of useful timing techniques is almost inexhaustible. Various methods are presented in other sections as appropriate examples are encountered. Each problem seems to have its own peculiarities, but there are certain clues which one can always look for. Once you realize that the exact timing appears to be too difficult to obtain, and the big O, order of magnitude, approach does not simplify the situation enough, there are several questions whose answers might give an insight into the timing problem. These include finding upper and lower bounds. Even if these bounds are not the **least upper bound (LUB) and greatest lower bound (GLB)**. As long as there appears to be some relation between the way the bound was determined and the timing of the function, the results can at least tell something about the range of timings that can be expected.

An upper bound reveals the worst timing one can expect and a lower bound shows the best timing. Just how relevant are these bounds? To determine the relevance of these bounds, attempt to construct a case that gives these

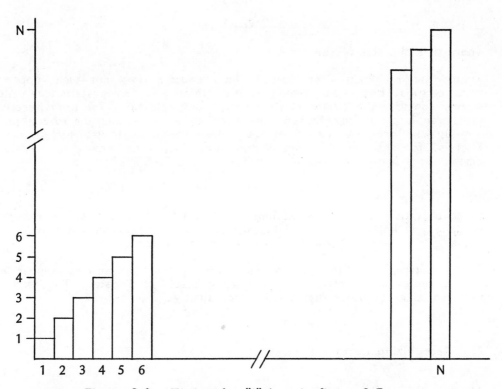

Figure 2.8.   Timing for "j" loop in figure 2.7

bounds, **a best case and a worst case.**   If best and worst cases can be found along with their timings, then GLB and LUB have been found.   Consider the program in figure 2.2.   If A [j] is always less than or equal to A [j+1] then the inner loop never executes and therefore the timing for any case that pro- duces this result would be a best case for the inner loop.   But that case is achieved only if the values in the array are all in order, and therefore, the best case is achieved for this loop and if at least one number is not in order, this best case is not achieved.

Occasionally, information about the bounds on the timing can be obtained in- directly by looking at **special cases** rather than specifically trying to find the LUB and GLB.   For example, since the timing of the inner loop in figure 2.2 depends upon the order of the values in the array, consider two special cases of that order, the numbers in correct order, and the numbers in reverse or- der.   The correct order case has already been mentioned above.   For the re- verse order case, count the number of loop iterations of the inner loop for each iteration of the outer loop.   The i-th time through the outer loop, the inner loop iterates i times, which is the maximum number of times it can iterate (because it iterates for j=i until j=0). With this we obtain the timing result

$$O(n^2/2)$$

where n is the size of the array.

Another approach uses statistics. This usually does not yield upper and lower bounds, but rather timing results which have some statistical validity. Again, consider the timing of figure 2.2, but this time, for each iteration of the inner loop, assume that **on the average** a value must be moved up half way up the array to get from its current position to its sorted position. That is, for the i-th iteration of the outer loop, the inner loop iterates i/2 times. This produces a timing result of

$$O(n^2/4).$$

Using a statistical approach assumes that you have some knowledge of statistics and you know that your data satisfies some statistical constraints, in particular, some known statistical distribution of the data.

Several examples of the use of statistics to time procedures appear later. The examples are restricted to uniformly distributed data. The techniques that are used for other distributions are similar.

2:6. Recognizing Certain Timings

Although a simple set of rules cannot be established to time all programs, there are certain timing situations that occur frequently and, when you know what to look for, these situations can be easily evaluated. Perhaps the most obvious grouping are sets of nested loops that lead to a polynomial timing,

$$O(c*n^k),$$

where c is some constant fixed by the algorithm, and k is the number of nested loops.

Consider the two sets of nested loops that appear in figure 2.9. These are two cases of nested loops where the number of iterations of the loops is controlled by one variable. In 2.9a, the k-loop depends upon j, the j-loop depends upon i, and the i-loop depends upon n, therefore, indirectly, all three loops depend upon the value in n. In 2.9b, the number of iterations of all three loops directly depend upon n. Obtain a time estimate for the k-loop in 2.9a using integration. This is given by the equation

```
FOR i = 1 TO n                        FOR i = 1 TO n
   FOR j = 1 TO i                        FOR j = 1 TO n
      FOR k = 1 TO j                        FOR k = 1 TO n

      { end of k loop }                    { end of k loop }

   { end of j loop }                     { end of j loop }

{ end of i loop }                     { end of i loop }

        (a)                                    (b)
```

Figure 2.9.   Two Loops with polynomial timing

$$T_a = O\left(\int_0^n \int_0^i \int_0^j dk \; dj \; di \right) = O(n^3/6) .$$

While the result for 2.9b is

$$T_b = O\left(\int_0^n \int_0^n \int_0^n dk \; dj \; di \right) = O(n^3) .$$

From this we see that the number of nestings governs the order of magnitude in those cases where the loops are governed by counters that increment through some range.   Given k nested loops governed by counters that increment additively to some value n, directly or indirectly, the loop timing is

$$O(n^k).$$

Changing the upper or lower limits of the range does not affect the order of magnitude as long as each loop has one limit which corresponds to the controlling variable (see the exercises).   Also note the effect of indirect control, figure 2.9a.   Usually this changes the timing only by a constant factor and this constant factor can be quickly approximated by the integration approach to obtaining a timing estimate.

Two other cases that frequently occur are illustrated in figure 2.10.   In figure 2.10a, the loop control variable, k, is multiplied by a constant factor each time the loop iterates.   In figure 2.10b, k is divided by a constant factor each time the loop iterates.   To time figure 2.10a, since k is initially 1, then after i loop iterations, the value in k is

```
k = 1                              k = n
WHILE k <= n DO                    WHILE k <> 0 DO

    k = incr*k                        k = k DIV 2

    { end of while loop }             { end of while loop }

        (a)                               (b)
```

Figure 2.10.   Logarithmic timed loops

$$INCR^i .$$

Assuming n is not changed as the loop iterates, then the loop performs i times until

$$INCR^i > n.$$

Taking the Log base INCR of both sides of this inequality produces

$$i > log_{INCR} n .$$

In figure 2.10b, k is initially set to the value in n, and each time the loop iterates, k is divided by 2 until k becomes zero. After i loop iterations, the value in k equals

$$n/2^i .$$

When 2^i becomes greater than n, then k becomes zero, that is,

$$2^i > n \quad or \quad i > log_2 n .$$

Generalizing from these observations, if the loop control variable is modified by multiplying or dividing by a constant value, b, and:

a.   If multiplied, the control variable is initially set to some value k and the loop terminates when the control variable becomes greater than some value n;

b.   If divided, the control variable is set to some value n and the loop terminates when the control variable is less than some value k,

```
FOR i = 1 TO n              j = 1
    j = i                  WHILE j <> n DO
    WHILE j <> 0 DO            FOR i = 1 TO j

        j = j DIV 2                { end i loop }

        { end of while }      j = 2*j

    { end of i loop }          { end of while loop }

        (a)                        (b)
```

Figure 2.11.   n log n loop structure

then the loop timing is

$$O(\log_b (\tfrac{n}{k})).$$

An obvious question is: What happens to a pair of nested loops when one whose control variable is additively incremented and the other whose control variable is multiplied, or divided? Two of these cases are illustrated in figure 2.11. The result in case 2.11a is given by the equation

$$\int_1^n \log i \; di = O(n \log n - n).$$

The solution to figure 2.11b is left for an exercise.

When should one consider a timing as being good? The graphs in figure 2.12 illustrate the relative growth rates of various timing functions. Obviously, given sufficient resources, one should try to write programs that perform in as little time as possible. The graph shows the relative desirability of various timings. First, observe the slow growth of logarithm functions. Logarithmic timing is desirable, unless an algorithm can perform in some small constant period of time or if another algorithm can be constructed which performs in less time, for example, log-log time.

The next slowest growth rates are linear growth functions, but close to them are the n log n timing functions. The polynomial functions are next and the lower the degree of the polynomial, the more desirable the timing. The growth rate of a polynomial times a log function is almost as desirable as the polynomial by itself. Observe the relation between the linear function and x*log x. x*log x at first looks like a linear function with a larger slope because it has very little curvature.

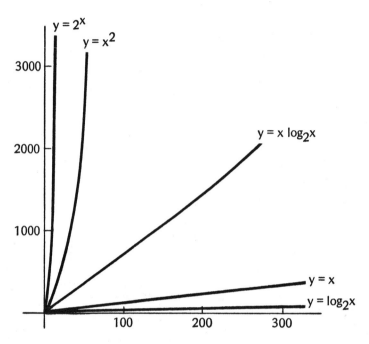

Figure 2.12.   Graph of various timing functions

There are some timing functions whose growth is dramatic and naturally, whenever possible, these timing functions should be avoided.   These are functions like

$$n!, \quad n^n, \quad \text{and} \quad e^n, \quad \text{or} \quad k^n$$

for some fixed k.   These timings are referred to as exponential timing functions because of their tremendous rates of growth.   In the example in figure 2.13, for each time through the i loop, the X loop iterates

$$i^i \quad \text{times.}$$

As i gets larger, the program time becomes intolerable.   Also, many programs with bad timing characteristics also have other problems which are beyond the scope of this text.

```
FOR i = 1 TO n
   aincr = 1.0/(i*i)
   x = 0
   WHILE x <= i DO

      x = x + aincr

   { end of while loop }

{ end of i loop }
```

Figure 2.13. An exponential timed loop structure

2:7. EXERCISES

1.   Determine the timings of the following loops.

```
FOR i = 1 TO n                      FOR i = 1 TO n
   FOR j = 1 TO n                      FOR j = i TO n
      FOR k = j TO n                      FOR k = i TO j

      { end of k loop }                  { end of k loop }

   { end of j loop }                   { end of j loop }

{ end of i loop }                   { end of i loop }

        (a)                                 (b)
```

2.   Determine the timings of the following loops.

```
FOR i = 1 TO n                      FOR i = 1 TO n
   FOR j = i TO n                      FOR j = n DIV 2 TO n
      FOR k = j TO n                      FOR k = 1 TO j

      { end of k loop }                  { end of k loop }

   { end of j loop }                   { end of j loop }

{ end of i loop }                   { end of i loop }

        (a)                                 (b)
```

3.   Determine the timings of the following loops.

```
k = 4                              k = 10000000
WHILE k <> n DO                       WHILE k >= 5 DO

    k = 9 * k                            k = k DIV 10

    { end of while loop }                { end of while loop }

        (a)                                  (b)
```

4.   Time the following loop structures.

```
FOR i = 1 TO n                     j = 2
    j = i                          WHILE j <= n DO
    WHILE j >= 2 DO                    FOR i = 1 TO j

        j = j DIV 5                        { end of i loop }

        { end of while loop }          j = 3*j

    { end of i loop }                  { end of while loop }

        (a)                                  (b)
```

3

Some Logical Structures

This chapter presents an intuitive description of several of the structures that are studied throughout this text. They are presented here **without re-**gard to their various representations. The reason being that, too often, programmers think of these structures in terms of specific representations. Actually most of these structures can be represented in many ways and the problem of choosing a structure and its appropriate representation is really two distinct problems:

1. Selecting the appropriate structures to represent and solve a problem;
2. Selecting the appropriate representation of the structure to fit into the problem's solution and resources.

While reading this chapter, one should make observations about the capabilities and limitations of each structure. The examples illustrate some of the classical uses of the structures.

3:1. Sequential Structures

Mention sequential structures and most programmers will immediately think of one dimensional arrays. Because of the ease with which it is represented in computer memories, it can be thought of as both a physical and a logical structure and can be described directly in terms of its basic representation. Intuitively, it consists of a sequence of memory locations with the following attributes:

1. All the locations in the array contain the same data type (integer, real, logical, etc], that is, it is homogeneous;
2. The locations can be **randomly accessed**, that is, the time required to access any location in the array is independent of the time required to access any other location (we are stuck, historically, with the term random access when perhaps the term independent access would be more appropriate);

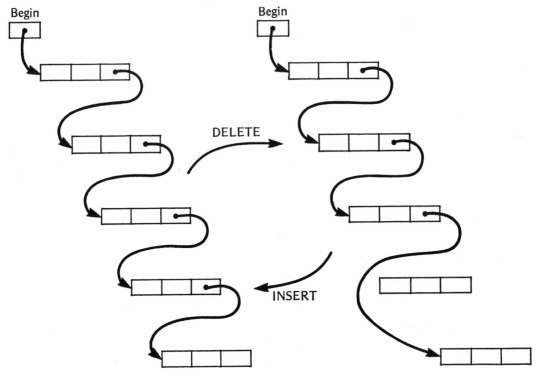

Figure 3.1. A visualization of a list - Insert and delete a record

3. The location (position), index, of any item in an array does not change because of the manipulation of other items in the array.

Normally, an array's size is fixed before data is placed into the array. When a fixed size is specified, an array of size n can be viewed as an ordered n-tuple and hence viewed as a **vector.** An **n-dimensional vector** or **ordered n-tuple** is a collection of numbers

$$V = (\, v_1, \, v_2, \, v_3, \, \ldots, \, v_n \,)$$

where two such vectors V and W are equal if and only if the dimensions of V and W are equal and

$$v_i = w_i$$

for all i, $1 \leq i \leq n$. That is, two vectors are equal if and only if they are the same size and contain the same values in each position.

Arrays are powerful, sometimes too powerful. For example, if an array is going to be processed sequentially, that is, item $J+1$ is accessed after item J, the random access property is more powerful than what is necessary for serial access. But sometimes an array is too weak. Consider an idealized file cabinet filled with folders. As new folders are inserted one simply pushes the other file folders aside to make room for new folders. This would be equivalent to inserting a new item into an array at some location in the array and the array would automatically adjust itself, in little or no time, to make space at the position where the new item is to be placed!

Gaining this capability at the expense of the random access property leads to the definition of a list. A **list** is a logical collection of data items which can be accessed serially and each item in the list can be a collection of data. Given access to any item in a list, depending upon the list type, access can be gained to the next item, and sometimes the previous item. This is discussed further when various list implementations are described in chapter 7. Besides serial access rather than random access, a list also has the property of expanding and contracting as items are inserted and deleted (think of an idealized file cabinet). As a file is inserted, room is made at little or no cost in time. As a file is removed, the other files come together to eliminate the space created in the position where the file was removed.

Figure 3.1 shows a typical method of visualizing a list as a collection of items. First, there is an indicator which locates the first item in the list. Along with each item in the list there is an indicator which locates the next item in the list. As an item is removed from a list (3.1a to 3.1b) the connecting information changes to eliminate the removed item from the list.

3:2. Sequential Structures with Very Limited Access

Consider a list structure with access limited only to the ends of the structure. That is, items may be inserted and deleted at the ends. Although such a structure might appear severely limited, two such structures play important roles in the manipulation of data. A **queue** is a sequential structure where items can be placed on one end and removed from the other. For orientation, call the removal end the front and the insertion end the rear. The order of items in a queue does not change. If one item is enqueued before another, it is dequeued before the second item. This is sometimes referred to as a **FIFO** organization, First In First Out.

There are several non-computer examples of queue organizations. The obvious ones are movie theater lines, lines at grocery store check out counters, etc. If you think of these lines in ideal situations, you can't sneak in, you must always go to the rear of the line, and you can't get out, except from

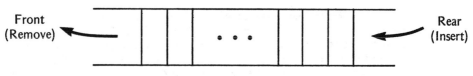

Figure 3.2.   The operations on a queue

the front of the line, then the concept of a queue applies.   Also, many vending machines hold their stock in queues.   For the vendor, this turns out to be a good way to store perishable goods.   Old stale products are dispensed from the machine while the fresh merchandise has a chance to become stale (Think about it).

A **pushdown stack,** or just stack for short, is a sequential structure where access is limited to only one end.   Items may be inserted or deleted from that one end and the stack expands or contracts accordingly.   The typical example of pushdown stacks is the storage devices for trays and plates in cafeterias. They function in such a way that only the dirty plate at the top can be easily accessed and the spring adjusts to the size of the stack as items are inserted or deleted.   This is referred to as a **LIFO** organization, Last In First Out.

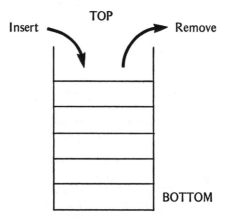

Figure 3.3.   A Pushdown Stack

Pushdown stacks are used so often in computing that it easy to include a computer oriented example.   There are two uses of stacks surrounding Polish

notation.   Polish notation is a method of writing arithmetic expressions
without using parentheses.   Actually, Reverse Polish Notation (RPN) is used
(no ethnic humor intended).   To illustrate, consider the expression

$$(A+B)*C .$$

In RPN, this is written as

$$A \; B \; + \; C \; *.$$

To write an infix expression in RPN, fully parenthesize the infix expression,

$$(A+B)*C = ((A+B)*C).$$

Now remove every left parenthesis, remove every operator, and replace every
right parenthesis by the operator that corresponds to it.   The result is the
RPN equivalent of the infix expression.

The meaning of an RPN expression is obtained by scanning the string from
left to right and as each operator is encountered perform that operation on
the two operands that are to the left of the operator and replace the operator
and operands by the result.

Assume A = 5, B = 9, and C = 4

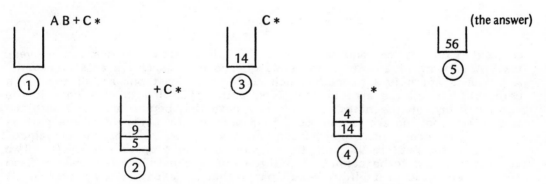

Figure 3.4.   Using a stack to evaluate A B + C *

Another way to describe the evaluation of reverse Polish expressions is by
using a stack.   Once again the RPN string is scanned from left to right and
two rules are used:

1. If the symbol being scanned is an operand, push it into the stack;
2. If the symbol is an operator, pop the top two items from the stack, perform the operation on them, and push the result onto the stack.

Figure 3.4 illustrates this use of a pushdown stack to evaluate AB+C* where A, B, and C equal 5, 9, and 4, respectively.

For completeness, a third structure must be mentioned, a double ended queue. A **double ended queue** is a sequential structure where an item may be inserted or deleted from either end. Description and use of this item is limited to several exercises.

3:3. Graphs

A graph can be intuitively thought of as a collection of points joined together by lines where the only "points" on each line, and hence in the graph, are the two points at the ends of the lines. The points on a graph are called **vertices, or nodes.** The lines are called **arcs.** Figure 3.5 illustrates an example of a graph. Note that only the indicated vertices are points on the arcs and although some arcs appear to intersect elsewhere, they do not. A good example of a graph would be the representations of the flight patterns of airlines. Although it appears as if the flights intersect, the only places where you can change planes are at the vertices, the airports.

There are certain standard terms that are used in graph theory and are meaningful in the way graphs are used in this text. A **path from one vertex to another** is a sequence of arcs

$$a_1, \ a_2, \ a_3, \ \dots, \ a_k$$

connecting the vertices and each sequential pair of arcs shares a common vertex. A **subpath** of a path is any subsequence of consecutive arcs in a path. A **proper subpath** is a subpath which contains at least one arc of the given path, but not all the arcs in the given path. The **length of a path** is the number of arcs in the path. A **cycle** is a path that begins and ends with the same vertex and no arc occurs more than once in the path. A **simple path** is a path that does not properly contain any cycles. "Properly contained" means that the path itself might be a cycle, but no subpath is a cycle. Two vertices are said to be **connected** if there exists a path between them. Each node is connected to itself by a null path, that is, a path of length zero. A **graph is connected** if every pair of vertices is connected.

Consider the graph in figure 3.5. There are many paths from vertex A to vertex E, for example, the sequence of arcs 2,4, or just the arc 6 is a path from A to E. The sequence of arcs 1,3,2,1,3,4 is a path from A to E but it is not a simple path because it contains a subpath (1,3,2) which is a cycle. This graph is not connected because there are no paths from any of the nodes A, B, D, and E to the nodes C and F.

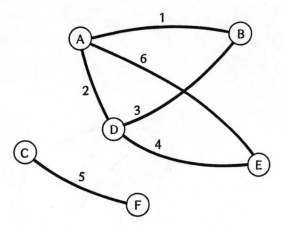

Figure 3.5. An example of a graph

Graphs in themselves are valuable and interesting structures, but most real world applications usually involve graphs where the vertices or arcs are labelled. For example, a graph of all the airline routes could have its arcs labelled with the flight numbers and the vertices labelled with the names of the airports.

Many classical problems and simplifications of real world problems that can be described and solved using graphs appear in the exercises. One example of such a problem is the four color problem. Simply described, the problem is: Given a map and only four colors, color the map in such a way that no two areas with a common border (Arizona and Utah do not have a common border, they meet at a point) are colored with the same color. The map can be represented as a graph with the role of the areas played by the vertices of the graph and when two areas have a common border, the common border is represented by an arc between corresponding vertices. Using this approach, the four color problem can be stated as a graph problem as follows: Label the vertices on the graph using only four different labels in such a way that two vertices with a common arc do not have the same label.

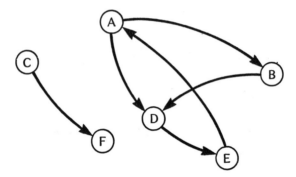

Figure 3.6. A Directed Graph

3:4. Directed Graphs

A Directed graph, or Digraph, is a graph in which the arcs are assigned directions. That is, rather than simply connecting two nodes, a direction is given to the connection. The arcs can be thought of as one way streets. All the graph theoretic terms from section 3.3 can be redefined to be used with directed graphs. For example, a **path in a directed graph from one node to another** consists of a sequence of arcs whose directions take us from the first node, to the next, and on to the last node. Because of the directions of the arcs, it is possible for one node to be connected to another but for the reverse not to be true. All the other definitions (cycle, simple path, connected graph, etc.) can be easily redefined for directed graphs.

Directed graphs have many applications which are used as exercises throughout this text. Digraphs are more general than graphs because of the directedness of the arcs. A digraph can represent a graph simply by having each arc of the graph being represented by two directed arcs of the digraph, one going in each direction. Although this might be viewed as an inefficient method of representing graphs, it illustrates the general capabilities of a digraph. The lack of examples of directed graphs is not due to their lack of use but rather because of the importance of the next subject, trees.

Figure 3.6 illustrates a digraph. Paths in digraphs are formed by sequences of arcs in which the end node of an arc in a path is the beginning node of the next arc in the path. For example, the sequence of arcs 1,3,4 is a path in the digraph of figure 3.6, but the sequence 4,3,1 is not a path. In a path in a digraph, all of the arcs in the path must be traversed in their indicated directions.

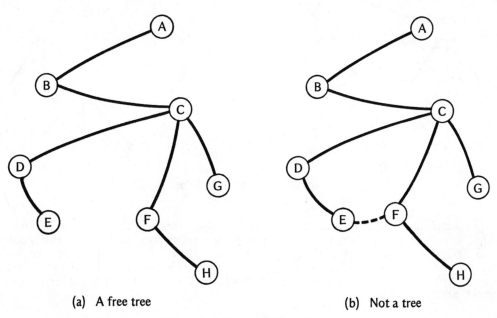

(a) A free tree   (b) Not a tree

Figure 3.7.   A Free Tree

3:5. Trees

Trees can be introduced by either using graphs or directed graphs. With graphs, a **free tree** is defined to be a connected graph that contains no cycles. That is, the path between any two nodes in a tree is unique. For example, the graph in figure 3.7a is a free tree, but the graph in figure 3.7b is not a tree because the additional arc between nodes E and F form a cycle (E to D to C to F to E).

Typically, one node is singled out and referred to as the **root node.** Once a
root is determined, the tree is referred to as a **rooted tree, or tree.** With a
root, all other nodes in the tree can be viewed relative to their position from
the root, hence the tree can be thought of as a digraph in which all arcs are
either directed towards or away from the root node.

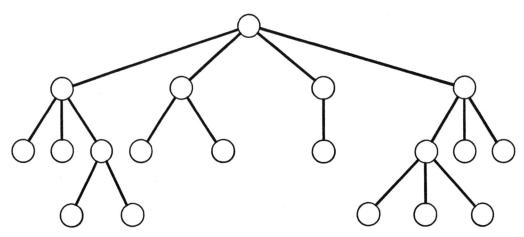

Figure 3.8. A Tree

Figure 3.8 illustrates a normal way of drawing trees with the root at the top.
The direction of the arcs is assumed to be from top to bottom and normally
the arrowheads are not inserted to indicate direction. Two nodes connected
by an arc are referred to as being in a **parent-child** relation. The node closest to the root is the parent. Two nodes with the same parent are referred
to as **siblings.**

Trees can be built within graphs and digraphs. **A spanning tree of a graph**
is a subgraph of a graph that is a tree and contains all the nodes of the
graph. The nodes that have no children are referred to as **leaves or terminal
nodes.** The arcs in a tree are called **branches.**

As the branches of a tree are traversed from the root to other nodes, the direct relation between two nodes connected by a branch is referred to as a
parent-child relation. One method of classifying trees is by counting the
maximum number of siblings any node might have. An **N-ary tree** is a tree in
which each node has at most N siblings. The simplest nondegenerate example
is a binary tree, each node has at most two siblings. Figure 3.9 is a binary
tree. Some nodes have no siblings, some have one, but no node has more
than two.

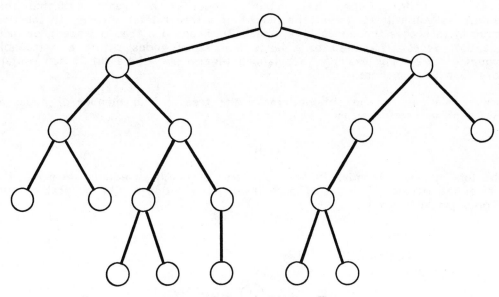

Figure 3.9.   A Binary Tree

The depth, or level, of a node in a tree is the length of the path between the node and the root. The height of a tree is the length of the longest path from the root. A tree is said to be **balanced** if all the leaves in the tree are at the same level. An obvious question concerning trees is: Given an n-ary tree of height h, what is the maximum number of nodes the tree can contain? Consider a balanced binary tree in which all non-terminal nodes, non-leaves, have exactly two children. Count the number of nodes at each level. At level zero, the root, there is only one node. At level one there are two nodes, at level two there are 4 nodes. At each level, there are twice as many nodes as at the previous level. If $N(J)$ is the number of nodes at level J, then we have the recursive relation $N(J) = 2*N(J-1)$. Since $N(0) = 1$,

$$N(J) = 2^J$$

for all J. If the height of the tree is H, then the number of nodes in the tree is

$$N(0)+N(1)+N(2)+ \ldots +N(H)$$

which equals

$$2^{H+1} - 1 .$$

If the tree is not balanced or if every non-terminal node does not have exactly two children, then the number of nodes in the tree is less than this value. As you will see later, the height of a tree relates directly to the time required to access the nodes in a tree. By keeping a tree balanced, or near balanced, access is gained to a large number of nodes within a reasonable amount of time. For example, a balanced binary tree of height 15 can contain more than 65000 nodes.

Similar relations can be obtained for n-ary trees. The number of nodes at level J of an n-ary tree is

$$n^J.$$

The total number of nodes in an n-ary tree of height h equals, at most, the sum of the number of nodes at each level. Derivation of the general formula is given as an exercise.

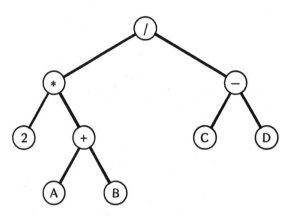

Figure 3.10.   An arithmetic expression as a tree

Figure 3.10 illustrates an arithmetic expression represented as a tree. In this example, the levels of the tree show us the precedence of the arithmetic operations and, therefore, the order in which the operations are to be performed. Figure 3.11 illustrates a tree containing words, a dictionary tree. With this tree, words are formed by copying the labels from the nodes as a path is traversed from the root to any marked node. The dictionary tree, as illustrated, contains the words "band", "bat", and "bad", but does not contain the word "ban", because that "n" node is not marked.

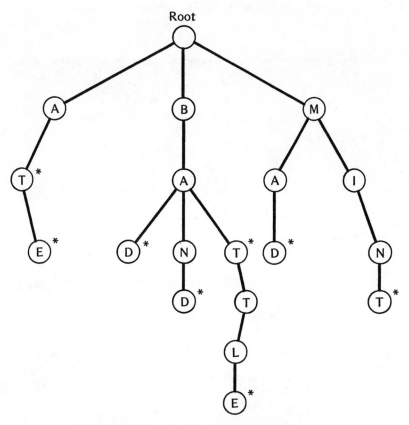

Figure 3.11.   A Dictionary Tree

3:6. EXERCISES

1. Draw a digraph representation of part of a map of your campus where the intersections are considered as nodes and the streets as arcs.

2. Draw a graphical representation of your house, or dormitory, in which all rooms and corridors are represented as vertices and all doorways as arcs.

3. Represent the quadratic formula as a tree.

4. Build a dictionary tree containing all of the words in this sentence including the words put, pit, pan, pant, paddle, puddle, and puppy.

5. Write the quadratic formula in RPN (Caution: Watch out for the unary minus and the unary square root function).   Use unique symbols for the unary functions and define appropriate stack actions for unary functions. Evaluate, using a pushdown stack, the expression

$$x^2 - x - 6.$$

6. Derive the formula for the maximum number of nodes in an n-ary tree of height h.

4

Queues and Stacks

Of the logical structures described in chapter 3, queues and stacks are perhaps the simplest, but the most used, structures. As you will see, many times, when working with more complex structures, a queue or stack helps to keep things organized. In this chapter several simple representations are described for these two structures. These simple representations are quite useful when only one queue or one stack must be implemented.

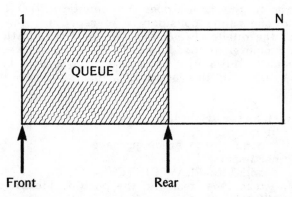

Figure 4.1. Representing a queue, front of queue - first array location

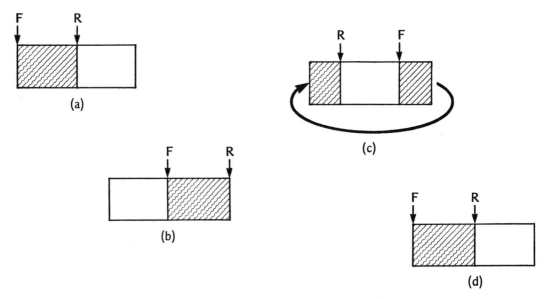

Figure 4.2. Wraparound representation of a queue

4:1. Queues

A **queue** is a sequential structure with limited access, namely, items can be inserted only at one end, the rear, deleted from the other, the front, and the order of items in the queue does not change, FIFO (first in, first out). A first approach one might consider is to represent the queue in an array with the front of the queue always kept in the first location of the array, see figure 4.1.   One pointer is used, REARPOINTER, to keep track of the last item in the queue.   Initially, the queue is empty.   This is indicated by REARPOINTER = 0.   With this approach, inserting new items is straightforward,

```
test to see if the array is full
if it is
    generate an error message
otherwise
    add 1 to REARPOINTER
    place the item into the position indicated by REARPOINTER
endif
```

However, the real problem with this apparently simple approach is the dequeuing process.   As an item is removed from the front of the queue, all other items in the queue must be moved forward.   This requires a loop and the loop executes in time O(size of queue).   Since the size of the queue is

```
1    PROGRAM nqdq (input, output);
2
3    TYPE
4        anarray = ARRAY [ 1 .. 5000 ] OF integer;
5
6    PROCEDURE nq (  item: integer;
7                    VAR   q: anarray;
8                    size: integer;
9                    front: integer;
10                   VAR rear: integer);
11
12       BEGIN
13       IF ( (rear+1) = front ) OR
14          ( (rear = size) AND (front = 1) ) THEN
15          writeln(' The queue is full')
16       ELSE
17          BEGIN
18          IF rear = size
19            THEN rear := 1
20            ELSErear := succ (rear);
21          q [rear] := item
22          END
23       END { of nq };
24
25   PROCEDURE dq ( VAR item: integer;
26                  VAR q: anarray;
27                  size: integer;
28                  VAR front: integer;
29                  rear: integer);
30
31       BEGIN
32       IF front = rear THEN
33          writeln(' The queue is empty')
34       ELSE
35          BEGIN
36          IF front = size
37            THEN front := 1
38            ELSE front := succ (front);
39          item := q [front]
40          END
41       END { of dq };
```

Figure 4.3. Enque and Deque algorithms for wraparound

variable, and sometimes might be quite large, this is undesirable.   Another
approach is needed,   one in which the enqueuing and dequeuing timings are
more manageable.

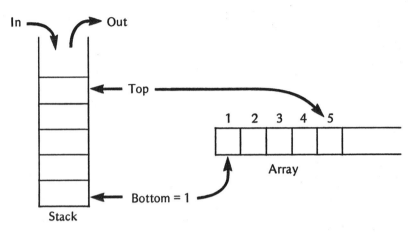

Figure 4.4. Stack in an array

An alternate approach is called **wraparound**. With this approach, two pointers
are used, call them FRONT and REAR. Initially,

$$0 < FRONT = REAR \leq \text{size of array}$$

to indicate that the queue is empty. Also, when FRONT = REAR during the
use of this approach, that indicates the queue is empty. Everytime an item
is enqueued, REAR is incremented and when items are dequeued, FRONT is
incremented. Whenever FRONT or REAR is incremented beyond the size of
the array, it is reset to one. Figure 4.2 illustrates a visual interpretation of
what is occurring. Algorithms to accomplish this appear in figure 4.3. Note
that even with the testing required for wraparound and other conditions, neither algorithm contains a loop.

In the enqueuing wraparound algorithm, a test is made to see if the array is
already full. At first, this might look as if the test is in error. However,
remember FRONT=REAR is the indication of an empty queue. If the test for
REAR+1=FRONT were not performed, then FRONT=REAR would indicate both a
full and an empty queue. By doing it this way, one location, the location
immediately preceding the front of the queue is not used. This means that
the space cost of this approach is 3 locations, the two pointers FRONT and
REAR and the one unused location in the array. However, the time for both
operations is constant so the tradeoff of time versus space is favorable.

The dequeuing algorithm begins by testing for an empty queue, then, if the
queue is not empty, an item is dequeued, then the FRONT pointer is reset according to the wraparound. Note that the FRONT pointer is reset **before the**
item is removed from the queue. This is because the FRONT pointer does not

point directly to the front of the queue. Actually, FRONT points to one before the beginning of the queue, therefore it must be incremented before the front of the queue can be accessed.

4:2. Pushdown Stacks

```
1    PROGRAM pushpop (input, output );
2
3    TYPE
4        anarray = ARRAY [ 1 .. 5000 ] OF integer;
5
6    PROCEDURE push (  item: integer;
7                    VAR stack: anarray;
8                    size: integer;
9                    VAR top: integer);
10
11       BEGIN
12       IF top = size THEN
13          writeln(' The stack is full ')
14       ELSE
15          BEGIN
16          top := top + 1;   stack [top] := item
17          END
18       END { of push };
19
20   PROCEDURE pop ( VAR item: integer;
21                  stack: anarray;
22                  size: integer;
23                  VAR top: integer);
24
25       BEGIN
26       IF top = 0 THEN
27          writeln(' The stack is empty ')
28       ELSE
29          BEGIN
30          item := stack [top];   top := top - 1
31          END
32       END { of pop };
```

Figure 4.5. PUSH and POP procedures for a stack in an array

Recall, a **pushdown stack, or stack,** is a sequential structure with limited access, namely, items may be inserted and deleted from only one end, called the **top of the stack,** and the position of items in the stack cannot change,

LIFO (last in, first out). A stack can be efficiently represented in an array using one pointer, call it TOP. In this approach, let the bottom of the stack be in location 1 of the array. An empty stack is indicated by TOP = 0.

```
1   PROGRAM quicksort (input, output);
2
3   TYPE
4      anarray = ARRAY [ 1..5000 ] OF integer;
5
6   PROCEDURE quick ( VAR a: anarray;
7                             n: integer);
8
9      TYPE
10        dset = (up, down);
11
12     VAR
13        direction: dset;
14        top, key, high, low, lowup, highdown: integer;
15        minst, maxst: ARRAY [ 1..20 ] OF integer;
16
17     PROCEDURE push ( first, second: integer);
18
19        BEGIN
20        top := top + 1;
21        minst [top] := first;
22        maxst [top] := second
23        END;
24      {  CONTINUED ON THE NEXT PAGE  }
```

Figure 4.5 contains algorithms to perform PUSH and POP operations on a stack represented in an array. Both algorithms are very direct. The PUSH algorithm must first test to see if the array is full, then if the array is not full, the TOP pointer is incremented and used to store the item. The POP algorithm first tests to see if the stack is empty, and if not, the item at the top of the stack is removed. In both cases, the space cost, beyond the size of the array, is one location for the pointer. Neither algorithm has any time dependence on the number of items in stack, or any other factors. That is, both algorithms function within a constant amount of time.

An example of the use of a pushdown stack appears in figure 4.6. This is a sort called a quicksort. This sort functions by picking a number, called the KEY, and finding the position where that number belongs. But, as the position is being found, the other numbers are moved so that all the numbers that are less than the KEY are placed ahead of the location where the KEY must be placed, and all the numbers greater than the key are placed after it. Therefore, in placing the KEY, the array is split into two other pieces that must be sorted and the numbers in one piece no longer have to be compared

```
25        BEGIN { of quick }
26           top := 0;  push ( 1, n );
27           WHILE top <> 0 DO
28              BEGIN
29              low := minst [top];  high := maxst [top];  top := top - 1;
30              IF low < high THEN
31                 BEGIN
32                 lowup := low;  highdown := high;
33                 direction := down;  key := a [low];
34                 WHILE lowup <> highdown DO
35                    BEGIN
36                    IF direction = down THEN
37                       IF key < a [highdown] THEN
38                          highdown := highdown - 1
39                       ELSE BEGIN
40                          a [lowup] := a [highdown];
41                          direction := up
42                          END
43                    ELSE
44                       IF key > a [lowup] THEN
45                          lowup := lowup + 1
46                       ELSE BEGIN
47                          a [highdown] := a [lowup];
48                          direction := down
49                          END
50                    END;
51                 IF (high - highdown) > (lowup - low) THEN
52                    BEGIN   push ( highdown + 1, high );
53                    push ( low, lowup - 1 )   END
54                 ELSE  BEGIN
55                    push ( low, lowup - 1 );  push ( highdown + 1, high )
56                    END
57                 END
58              END
59        END { of quick };
```

Figure 4.6.   A Quicksort Procedure

to the numbers in the other piece.   Now, these two pieces must be sorted. As one piece is sorted, a pushdown stack saves information that indicates the location of the other piece.   But as the one is sorted, it too is split into two pieces that must be sorted, etc., etc.   Hence the pushdown stacks are used to keep track of those pieces that must still be sorted.   The pushing process continues until the pieces are broken down into single items and hence need not be sorted.

The algorithm functions as follows: A pair of pointers indicate the beginning and end of the piece of the array that is to be sorted, HIGH and LOW. These are popped from the stacks MINST and MAXST.   Two pointers, lowup and highdown, are used in the sorting and placing of the KEY. The KEY is taken from A [LOW]. Locating the position of the KEY is done in the inner loop by switching back and forth between the following two processes until **lowup = highdown**. First, highdown is decremented until an item is found that is less than the key. When, and if, one is found, it is moved to the location indicated by lowup. Second, lowup is incremented until an item is found that is greater than the key. When, and if, one is found, it is moved to the location indicated by highdown.

Figure 4.7 illustrates the effect on an array of one iteration of the outer loop of the program in figure 4.6. The 36 in location one becomes the KEY value and location one becomes available (figure 4.7a). Highdown is now decremented until it points to a value that is less than the key value (figure 4.7b), and this value is moved to the position indicated by lowup. The location indicated by highdown is now vacant and lowup is now incremented until it points to a value greater than the KEY value (figure 4.7c). This process continues until lowup = highdown, then the KEY value is placed back into the array at that position indicated by both pointers (figure 4.7d). The number 36 is now in its correct postion because all values less than it are below it in the array and all values greater than it are above it in the array.

When the inner loop terminates, the KEY is placed into the array and the information about the two pieces of the array that must be sorted are pushed into the stacks. The order in which the information is pushed into the stacks is important because it affects the potential sizes of the stacks. The items must be pushed so that the pointers to the larger sequence of numbers must be pushed first. By pushing the pointers to the larger piece first, the smaller piece is processed first.

By processing the smaller piece first, the stack size can be limited. This can be seen by looking at one special case, namely, assume that the numbers are already in sorted order. Then the KEY would always be placed back where it was. The "two pieces" that must be sorted are really just one piece, the rest of the array, and a null piece. If the null piece was pushed first, and this process continued, then the sizes of the stacks would have to be the same as the size of the original array and the space costs would be

$$O(2 * \text{size of the array}).$$

This is not desirable.

Consider the approach where the pointers are pushed into the stack, with the pointers for the larger piece pushed first. The worst case for stack sizes occurs when the KEY exactly divides the array in two. As the array is divided in two, one of these pieces is divided in two, etc., etc., this process continues k times until

$$2^k \geq \text{size of the array} .$$

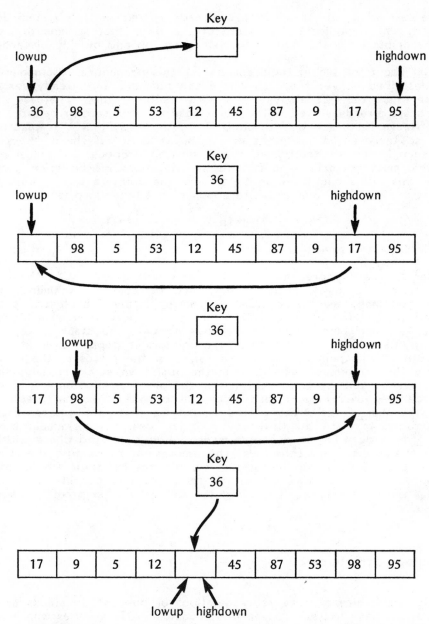

Figure 4.7. One iteration of the inner loop of Quicksort

This gives k = O(log (array size)). Actually, k = INT(log(array size)) + 1.
This means that stacks of 16 locations can handle arrays of 32768 positions.

For the case where the numbers are already sorted, only two stack locations are used, one to indicate the extent of the piece that remains to be sorted with the pointers for the null piece pushed on top and quickly discarded.

But what about the timing requirements for this procedure? Consider the two cases described above, the case where the numbers are already sorted, and the case where the KEY always fits exactly in the middle. The case when the numbers are already sorted is the worst case for this sort procedure. To see this, observe that each time through the outer loop, a KEY is placed in the array, so there are n iterations of the outer loop. If the numbers are already sorted, the ith iteration of the outer loop produces a piece of n-i locations that must be sorted and it takes n-i iterations of the inner loop to determine this, plus one iteration to discard the pointers to the null piece of the array. The total number of iterations of the inner loop is

$$n + (n-1) + (n-2) + \ldots + 2 + 1$$

which is $O(n^2)$. Proving this is the worst case is left as an exercise.

Consider the case where the KEY is always placed exactly in the middle of the piece of the array being sorted. To determine this timing, use the graphic approach, see figure 4.8. As shown, figure 4.8 illustrates the time required to sort log n keys. This timing is important in that during this process, as each pair of pointers is pushed onto the stack a key value is placed in the array and only one of the pointers is popped to locate the next key. But at this point, we know the sizes of the pieces of the array indicated by the pointers at each level in the pushdown stack, namely, the piece at one level is at least twice the size of the piece stacked on top of it. The time order required to sort each piece can be placed on our graph, as follows: the sum of the areas of the rectangles in figure 4.8 represents the time required to place the first key. Under ideal circumstances, those rectangles fit inside a larger rectangle whose height is N and whose width is log N. As the sort process continues, the timings for processing the information that has been pushed into the stacks will fill this rectangle (under ideal circumstances). In this way the entire rectangle can be filled and the time $O(n*\log n)$ result follows. Providing the details of this proof is given as an exercise.

4:3. Multiple Structures

Although these simple array representations of queues and stacks are valuable, they do have limits. To see this, consider several cases where it is desirable to implement more than one of these structures simultaneously. If space is critical, one cannot just go ahead and implement each structure in a separate array. For example, suppose two queues must be represented in 1000 memory locations. Further, during program execution, at various times each queue contains more than 500 items.

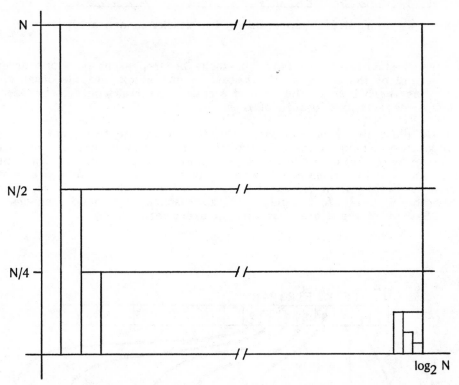

Figure 4.8.   Timing graph for quicksort on a special case

A solution is to represent both queues in one array using wraparound and have the two queues follow each other around the array.   That is fine as long as the amount of enqueuing and dequeuing from each queue remains the same during the execution of the program.   But suppose the one queue is used more often than the other?   Then the one queue will bump into the other queue.   Now what should be done?

But before tackling this problem, there is at least one multiple structure implementation that is convenient, namely, the simultaneous representation of two pushdown stacks.   This is a common problem in computing because of the

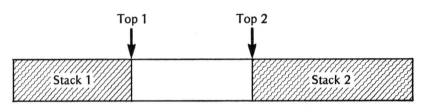

Figure 4.9.   Representing two stacks in one array

many uses of stacks.   Two pushdown stacks are represented in one array by using one end of the array as the bottom of one stack and the other end of the array as the bottom of the second stack.   The free space is between the two stacks and available to both of them.

Figure 4.9 illustrates this approach.   In this way, the two stacks can grow independently, as long as there is enough space available in the array.   However, using an array to represent two queues does present us with a bumping problem.   This problem arises when information passes through one of the queues more rapidly than it passes through the other queue.   It is an interesting problem, but unfortunately most approaches only handle special situations.   Several of these are described in exercises.

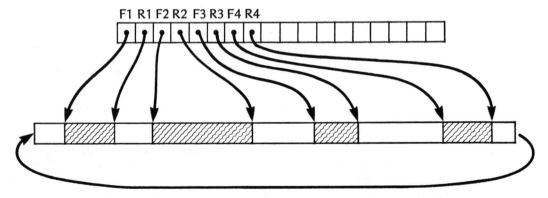

Figure 4.10.   Two array approach for representing multiple queues

Other limitations of this approach can be readily seen if you must simultaneously represent a queue and a pushdown stack.   Or consider this hypothetical problem: You are asked to write routines which implement several queues simultaneously in one array. However, the exact number of queues will not be specified until the program executes. At first one might consider the first approach illustrated in figure 4.10. With this approach, two small arrays and one large array are used. The two small arrays contain the pointers to the locations containing the queues, which are all in the one large array. Then, besides the NQ and DQ routines, an INITQ routine would be used. The INITQ routine would be called once to initialize the allocation and inform the procedures as to how many queues are being used. From there on the queues would all be implemented using wraparound and except for the bumping problem, everything looks fine. One obvious problem is that the two small arrays must be larger than or equal to the number of queues being allocated. But if they are larger, then some of the space in the smaller arrays is wasted because it will not be used although it might be needed in the larger array because of the amount of information that the queues must hold.

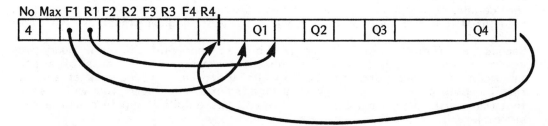

Figure 4.11. One array approach for representing multiple queues

Rather than wasting that space, the illustration in figure 4.11 demonstrates another alternative, namely, putting everything into just one array and using pointers to keep track of everything. With this approach, the INITQ routine allocates the array and separates it into two parts as illustrated. This might be accomplished with a procedure

INITQ (ARRAY, SIZE, NUMQ)

which sets up the array as shown in the illustration. Then the routines NQ(QNUM, ITEM) and DQ(QNUM, ITEM) would access the appropriate queue.

Some of the problems that come up, in particular the bumping problem, would be handled in the NQ routine by a call to a BUMP routine. Also, recognizing an empty queue and determining when a bump occurs are interesting problems that are given in the exercises. At this point, you should think about how you would program some of these routines. One observation you should make is that as you design and code a procedure, what you gain in terms of real capabilities is not that great when compared to the programming effort put into the problem. Also, suppose it is a mixture of stacks and queues that

must be represented.   Now there is definitely a bumping problem.   At this
point, it should become fairly obvious that this approach represents an apparent dead end and another approach should be considered when multiple
queues and stacks are required to solve a problem.

4:4. Review

At this point, it is good to reflect on certain things that were mentioned earlier.   First, one must not confuse the logical requirements of a program with
the physical details of carrying out the program.   When a programmer finds
that implementational details begin to overwhelm the programming project, it is
a good indication that something is wrong, either with the approach or with
its implementation.   For example, by taking the simple approaches of representing one queue or one stack in an array and trying to generalize it into
representing multiple queues or stacks in an array, one gets bogged down in
the details of manipulating the array.   Remember, an array is a physical
structure, it is not a queue or a stack.   They are logical structures.

Second, a difficult thing to recognize, but an important thing for good programmers and system designers to observe is when the rewards of a programming effort are worth the cost of the approach.   If you look at some of
the "bumping problems" and try to design solutions to them, you will observe
that many little details must be handled and the details begin to consume considerable amounts of time.

But why all this concern about time?   The answer is that here we are talking
about some of the simple elementary routines that more complex programming
systems are going to use.   The complex system will have its own time problems.   If these are compounded by the timings of the elementary data handling routines, the system could become useless because of the amount of
computer time required by the elementary routines in the programming system.

Why should we be concerned about memory space?   Many of the computers
available today have megabytes of memory. Why be concerned with 10, 50, or
even 100 memory locations?   There are so many answers to this question.   On
a high plane, the answer is pride of workmanship.   A program is a work of
art!   Although there might be one or more layers of systems interface between your program and the computer, concern for time and memory allocation
can save real time and real computer resources when your program executes.
A few extra memory locations can mean the difference in the way an operating
system places your program in memory.   This can mean better resource allocation for your program and can translate into a lower cost of execution or
less wall clock time (actual time spent in the system by your program).

One final observation must be made.   Note the use of pointers.   They help
and their cost in terms of time and space is minimal when compared to what

they do for us. The value of pointers, that is, variables that are not elementary data but are used to tell where data is located, become more useful as our approach towards representing information becomes more sophisticated.

4:5. EXERCISES

1. Prove that the timing case when the data is already sorted is the worst case for the quicksort.

4. Prove the case when the KEY is continually placed into the middle of the remaining piece produces the best case for the quicksort procedure.

3. What is the timing of the quicksort if the numbers are in reverse order?

4. Write routines that use a pushdown stack to translate fully parenthesized strings into reverse Polish notation (RPN).

5. Write routines that use a pushdown stack to evaluate arithmetic expressions written in RPN.

6. Write a program to simulate a queue at a movie theater ticket booth. Start your program by placing a random number of parties in the queue with each party consisting of between 2 and 7 people. The time it takes to process (dequeue) a party is 7*p seconds where p is the size of the party. Assume that parties, of random size as described above, arrive according to the following schedule:

   1. Every IRAND(58) seconds for the first 20 minutes;
   2. Every IRAND(30) seconds for the next 20 minutes;
   3. Every IRAND(100) seconds for the last 20 minutes.

   How many parties are processed? What is the largest size of the queue? What is the smallest size of the queue? What is the maximum number of people waiting in the line? IRAND (n) is assumed to be an integer pseudorandom number generator satisfying the condition

   $$0 <= IRAND (n) < n.$$

7. Complete the details of the proof that the best time for the quicksort is $O(n \log n)$.

8. Write routines NQ, DQ, and BUMP, where BUMP might be called by NQ, which simulates two queues in one array. The BUMP procedure should determine the amount of available space and reposition the bumped queue so that the available space uniformly separates the two queues.

9. Write INITQ, NQ, DQ, and BUMP for the second approach towards representing multiple queues in one array. Carefully describe the things that BUMP must do to carry out its task.

10. Write the routines NQ, DQ, INITQ, and BUMP for representing several queues in one array using the second approach. Write BUMP so that it might be called by NQ as required.

11. Since the front pointer actually points to one before the front of each queue and the queue pointers are also kept in the array, if the array is of size M and N queues are implemented, how much actual space is available for data?

12. Determine the time problems encountered with the BUMP algorithm.

5

Pointers and
Dynamic Allocation

Pointer variables provide a fundamental approach for carrying out a variety of data structure problems. But they gain their value through the "random access" capability of computer memories and the ability to mix various data types in memory. The ability to mix data types leads to the concept of records. That is, a collection of items of mixed types which have some logical relation and are kept physically together in memory.

5:1. Memory Access

A critical element in the efficiency of programs is the speed and appropriateness of the devices that contain the data as well as the way the data is organized. Although the type and speed of storage devices change, there are certain general observations that can be made about the limitations and the appropriateness of different devices.

An important component in a computer is its primary memory. Here the term random access describes the way memory is accessed by the CPU. Although we are stuck with the term "random access", a more appropriate term would be independent access. By this we mean that it takes at most some small fixed amount of time (normally at most a few microseconds) to access a memory location regardless of:

1. The actual address of the location being accessed;
2. The location of the last memory location accessed;
3. The location of the instructions performing the access or any other possible factor.

The importance of the access capabilities of the primary memory of a computer system can be appreciated when it is compared to the speed and abilities of other devices. For example, consider two widely used storage media, magnetic tapes and magnetic disks. Although both of these storage media are important, they both lack the independent access character of main memory.

To see this, consider magnetic tapes. If the information that is to be accessed is a certain distance along the tape from the tape unit's read/write head, the time required to read the information depends upon both the distance of the data from the read/write head and the speed of the tape drive. Although the speed of tape drives and the density of information can change the time required to access data, the fact remains that the access time is dependent upon the relative position of the information on the tape.

Disk drives are often erroneously referred to as random access devices. This is often done by equipment vendors in order to present disks as a rapid access storage device. Disks are a fast and flexible storage medium, but the access of information on a disk does depend upon factors which can influence the efficiency of a program. On a movable head disk drive, information is stored in concentric circular tracks. The disks spin at a constant rate. The read/write heads must be positioned above a track for information to be read from or written to a track. To access information on a disk the read/write head must be positioned above the appropriate track, then the hardware must wait for the information to pass by the read/write head. Therefore, the time to access information on a disk, among other things, is dependent upon the position of information relative to the position of the read/write head, which in turn depends upon the location of the last data that was accessed.

Although memory access is something that is taken for granted, it is brought up at this point for two reasons. First, the random access property (or independent access property as we would prefer to call it) allows us to perform a variety of data structure techniques in good time. Second, when various data structure methods have to be carried out using other storage devices, both the appropriateness of the devices and the device's access dependence must be considered. These considerations are discussed in Chapter 14.

5:2. Records

Arrays are physically sequential homogeneous collections of data. All items in an array are of the same type. Sometimes, it is desirable for information to be logically kept together although the items of information are not all the same types. For example, an array of characters might contain a person's name, an integer variable for a social security number, a boolean variable to indicate marital status, and a real variable to contain some other related information. Since the information is logically related, it might be advantageous to keep it physically together. This is the purpose behind the intuitive concept of records.

A record is a heterogeneous physically sequential structure which contains information that has some logical relation and can be conveniently accessed either as a unit or each item in the record can be accessed separately. Several programming languages provide a variety of different types of support for records. Rather than getting involved with the idiosyncrasies of these various methods, the simplest approach meets the purpose of this text. Here, the notation to define and access records is that used in PASCAL.

A record is a type of memory allocation. In PASCAL, a record type is defined by listing the names and the type of the components within a record.
For example,

```
TYPE
     employee = RECORD
                     name: PACKED ARRAY [ 1..20 ] of CHAR;
                     ssno: 0..999999999;
                     married: BOOLEAN;
                     other: REAL
                     END;
```

would define the record type mentioned above. Then

```
          VAR
             joe,sam: employee;
```

defines two records named "joe" and "sam". The components in the records
are accessed by stating both the record and the component in the record.
For example, to indicate "joe" is married,

```
          joe.married := TRUE.
```

One consideration that is bypassed here is the efficient allocation of records.
The fact is that many computer systems have different requirements with regard to the amount of memory and the positioning for various data types.
Since a record can typically contain different data types, the actual amount of
memory allocated to a record might be more than just the sum of the allocations of the record's components. This is due to memory boundary requirements of some computer systems. However, these are hardware/software considerations that vary from one computer system to another.

Typically, as is the case in PASCAL, the memory allocation is done with an
eye towards time efficiency. That is, normally, the allocation of records is
made for convenient instruction execution. Timing results obtained in this
text assume this to be the case.

5:3. Pointer Variables and Dynamic Records

The concept of pointers is quite simple. In general, pointers are address information. The name of a variable becomes a pointer to the memory location
that contains the information that corresponds to that variable. An array index is a **relative pointer**. That is, indices, or subscripts, locate the position
of information within an array. Early use of relative pointers was presented
in chapter 1 with the INDEXSORT and LINKSORT procedures. In these two
procedures, the arrays INDEX and LINK, respectively, contained relative

pointers which assisted in performing the sort without actually moving the data.

The next step is to replace the relative pointer information in these arrays to actual hardware address information. A **pointer variable** is a variable type that can contain only address information. Programming languages provide various means of support to pointer variables. Once again, the notation of PASCAL is used here. If POINT is to be a pointer variable to data of type T, then the notation to describe this is

> TYPE
>   link =↑T;
>
> VAR
>   point:link.

Pointer variables have their greatest versatility when used for dynamic allocation. For example, since POINT, defined above, can point to data of type T, then new data space can be allocated during the execution of the program. In PASCAL, this would be accomplished by

> new(point).

If "point" is a pointer variable, then

> point↑

accesses the type T data space that is indicated by "point". The space indicated by "point" can be released. That is, it can be returned to the space allocation procedure through the dispose procedure,

> dispose(point).

Details and alternatives to the new and dispose procedures are discussed in more detail in chapter 14.

The full richness of pointer variables can be seen if they are combined with RECORDs that contain components which are pointer variables to other records of the same type. In this way, as a program executes, an arbitrary number of records can be dynamically allocated while the program executes. With this ability, it is not necessary for a programmer to preallocate all the data space. Rather, as a program executes, it can allocate the space it needs.

Figure 5.1 illustrates a way of visualizing the use of pointers and records. If X is a pointer to records and records contain two components, an integer data component and a pointer component, then

> X↑.DATA

indicates the value in the record pointed to by X, while

$$X\uparrow.POINT\uparrow.DATA$$

indicates the value in the record after that. The pointers indicate the logical sequencing of the records regardless of their actual physical locations.

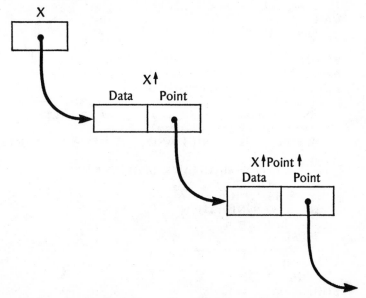

Figure 5.1. An abstraction of pointers and records

5:4. A Dynamic Allocation Example

In chapter 1, the LINKSORT procedure comes close to demonstrating the way pointer variables are used. In that procedure, see figure 1.7, the array LINK and the variable HEAD play the role of pointer variables except that they actually contain array indices. To illustrate the relation between this earlier "simulation" of pointer variables to the actual use of pointer variables, consider the program in figure 5.2.

```
 1    PROGRAM pointersort (input, output, unsorted);
 2
 3    TYPE
 4        link = ↑item;
 5        item = RECORD
 6                    data: integer;
 7                    point: link
 8               END;
 9
10    VAR
11        unsorted: text;
12
13    PROCEDURE
14        linksort2 ( head: link );
15
16        VAR
17            prev, this, n: link;
18
19        BEGIN
20        head := NIL;   reset(unsorted);
21        WHILE NOT eof(unsorted) DO
22            BEGIN
23            this := head;  new ( n );  prev := NIL;
24            read (unsorted, n↑.data);
25            WHILE (this <> NIL) AND (n↑.data > this↑.data) DO
26                BEGIN
27                prev := this;   this := this↑.point
28                END;
29            n↑.point := this;
30            IF prev = NIL THEN
31                head := n
32            ELSE
33                prev↑.point := n;
34            readln
35            END
36        END;
```

Figure 5.2.   LINKSORT using pointers and records

This procedure, LINKSORT, is a direct translation of the earlier LINKSORT procedure in figure 1.7.   The word NIL is used to set a pointer variable with no address or test it for no address.   This procedure is written assuming that the unsorted values are in a file rather than in an array.   Each time through the outer loop,

NEW(N)

allocates records with N pointing to the new record.   Then a value is read into the DATA component of that record.   The inner loop then determines the

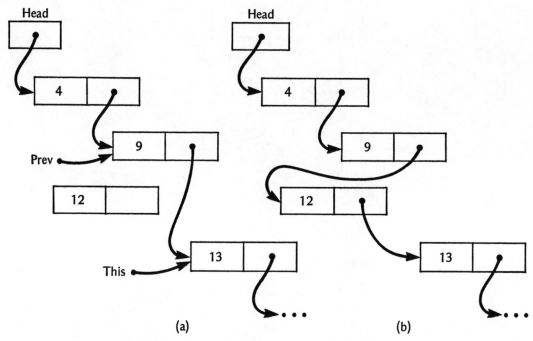

Figure 5.3.   Insertion in an ordered list

proper position in the logical sequencing by setting the pointers in PREV and THIS to point to the two records that contain the two values that bracket the value N↑.DATA, see figure 5.3a.   As the inner loop terminates, N↑.POINT is set to point to the record pointed to by THIS.   The IF-ELSE structure determines one of two possibilities. If PREV = NIL, then the inner loop never executes.   This means that N↑.DATA is the smallest value seen thus far, therefore, HEAD must be set to point to this record.   Otherwise, the pointer PREV↑.POINT is set to point to the record indicated by N to properly position this record between the two records indicated by the pointers PREV and THIS, see figure 5.3b.

6

Lists

Lists were described in general in chapter 3. Here two representations are described. The first method is one-way vs. two-way lists. One-way lists seem to serve a very useful purpose and only occasionally does the added memory overhead pay for itself with a two-way representation. The second method is circular vs. ground lists. Ground lists are easy to work with, but although circular lists appear on the surface to cause algorithm development problems, procedures that work on ground lists can be relatively easily adapted to circular lists.

6:1. Ground One-Way Lists

Lists are logically sequential collections of information. They can be easily represented with dynamic records where each record, besides containing the data that corresponds to that position in the list, also contains a pointer to the next record in the list. The pointers can be placed anywhere in records. The position of the pointer in the list is not important. The pointer, like any other item in a record, is accessed by its name. Where the name is placed in the record description is irrelevant. For consistency, the pointer happens to be the first displacement mentioned in record descriptions for procedures in this chapter. No significance should be placed on the fact that the pointer is the first item mentioned in the record. The pointer can be anywhere in the record.

A list is **one-way** means that each record in the list contains one pointer to the next record in the list. A **ground list** is a list representation in which the pointer in the last record of the list is null. The term "list" shall be used to mean a one-way grounded list. Later, as other types of lists are defined, their qualifications are used when naming those other types of lists (e.g. circular list). Null pointers are usually represented by placing a value that cannot be a valid pointer into a pointer variable. Typically, pointers are address information and addresses are generally integer values greater than or equal to zero. Normally, a particular value is chosen as a null, 0,

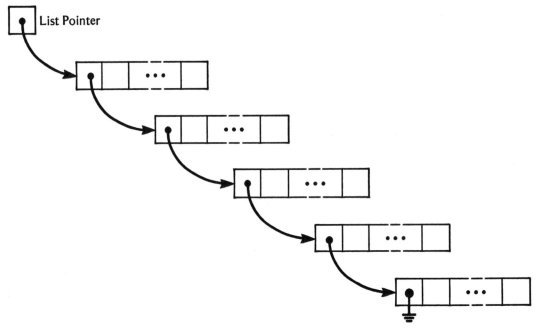

Figure 6.1. Abstraction of records in a List

-1, or some other value and used consistently in this way. Sometimes the choice of a null depends upon the particular system you are using. Here the word null is used and no further assumptions are made about its value except that it is a valid null for your system.

One-way grounded lists provide one-way sequential access to a collection of information. An immediate application of one-way grounded lists is the representation of pushdown stacks. To illustrate this, consider the algorithms in figure 6.2. Assume that **new** and **dispose** are procedures to allocate and release dynamic records. Also, assume that each location in the stack contains only one data item. Then, the stack is kept as a one-way grounded list and a pointer to the first item in the list, which represents the top of the stack, provides access to the list. Call this pointer, STACK, and assume that originally STACK is set to the null value to indicate an empty stack. The PUSH procedure allocates a dynamic record, places the data item in that record, and relinks the list with the new data item at the front of the list to indicate that it is at the top of the stack. The POP operation first checks to make sure that STACK is not null, then it removes the data item from the first dynamic record in the list, relinks the list to remove the first record, then **dispose** releases the unlinked dynamic record.

```
1    PROGRAM stackinlist (input, output);
2
3    TYPE
4        link = ↑item;
5        item = RECORD
6                    point: link;
7                    data: integer
8                 END;
9
10   PROCEDURE
11       push ( VAR stack : link;
12             val : integer );
13
14       VAR
15           top : link;
16
17       BEGIN
18       new ( top ); top↑.data := val;
19       top↑.point := stack;    stack := top
20       END { of push };
21
22   PROCEDURE
23       pop ( VAR stack : link;
24             val : integer );
25
26       VAR
27           oldtop : link;
28
29       BEGIN
30       IF stack = NIL THEN
31           writeln(' ATTEMPT TO POP EMPTY STACK')
32       ELSE
33           BEGIN
34           oldtop := stack;    val := oldtop↑.data;
35           stack := oldtop↑.point;    dispose ( oldtop )
36           END
37       END { of pop };
```

Figure 6.2.   PUSH and POP procedures for a stack kept as a list

There are two advantages to this approach. First, both the PUSH and POP operations function within a fixed constant amount of time. That is, there is no unusual time overhead due to dynamic allocation unless the **new** and **dispose** routines cost some unknown large amount of time. Ways of implementing **new** and **dispose** are discussed in chapter 12. Second, no assumptions are made about any predetermined limitations on the size of the stack due to limitations in any preallocated arrays. The only limitations are limitations due to the space that might be available to **new** and **dispose**. This means, assuming the time costs of **new** and **dispose** are reasonable, this approach yields similar

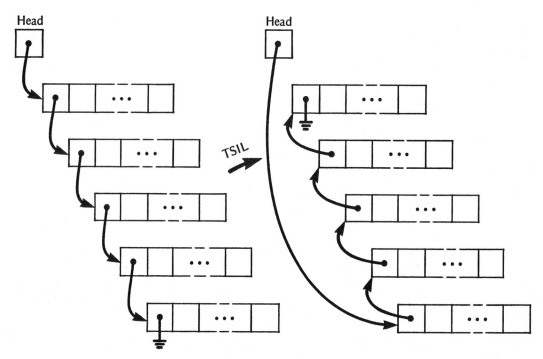

Figure 6.3.   Reversing the links in a list

timing without the predefined limitations that existed when stacks were represented with arrays.

However, the PUSH and POP algorithms do not gain this advantage for free. Each dynamically allocated record contains a pointer to the next record in the list. Assuming each data type uses the same size memory location, 50% of the space is being used to store pointers! Is this 50% space cost worth it? At this point, this might look like a real dilemma. However, suppose each position in the stack was used to store 2 data items. Then 2/3 of the dynamically allocated space would be used for data. This could be the case for the quicksort, since two items are stored and retrieved together. However, the simple array allocation scheme for the stacks in the quicksort appear to be sufficient. Recall from section 2.3, that 2 stacks can be efficiently implemented in one array. But the implementation of three or more stacks creates a problem for space allocation. By implementing the stacks as lists, each with their own pointer, the stacks can be dynamically allocated without any concern for predefined array sizes forcing limitations on the size of any stack. All the stacks have the same access to the dynamically allocated space and a program using this approach would fail only when the storage management routines fail (see 12:3).

```
1     PROGRAM groundtsil (input, output);
2
3     TYPE
4         pointer = ↑listrec;
5         listrec = RECORD
6                        link : pointer;
7                        data : integer
8                    END;
9
10    PROCEDURE tsil ( VAR list : pointer );
11
12        VAR
13            previous, current, next : pointer;
14
15        BEGIN
16        previous := NIL;  current := list;
17        WHILE current <> NIL DO
18            BEGIN
19            next := current↑.link;
20            current↑.link := previous;
21            previous := current;
22            current := next
23            END;
24        list := previous
25        END;
```

Figure 6.4. The TSIL procedure

Once a list is created, can the links of the list be changed so that the direction of the list is reversed? Figure 6.3 illustrates the desired action. This
action can be accomplished by a very compact algorithm, see figure 6.4. The
algorithm, called TSIL (that's LIST spelled backwards), performs this task by
stepping through the list, one record at a time, and changing the pointer in
the record so that it points to the record that used to precede it. The
pointer variables in the algorithm, PREV, etc., hold the pointers in order so
that the relinking process can be accomplished. This algorithm performs
within a reasonable amount of time. Since a list of n records would require
that n pointers must be changed, the best that can be expected is time O(n).
The algorithm contains one loop and the number of times this loop iterates
depends linearly upon the size of the list. Therefore, the algorithm functions
in time O(n), which is as good as we can expect.

One-way grounded lists do have limitations. First, they cannot be used to
efficiently represent queues. This is investigated further as an exercise.
Second, the natural limitations due to one-way sequential access carry over to
lists. For example, suppose you wish to access a record in the list, then
that record contains a count of the number of the record preceding it that is
really supposed to be accessed. A backtracking, or two-way linkage would

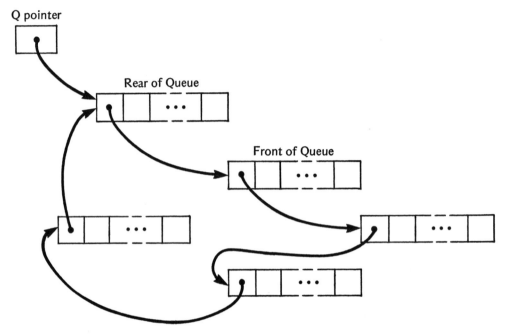

Figure 6.5. Using a circular list to represent a queue

be ideal, but that cannot be done without using either additional memory, or additional, $O(n)$, time.

6:2. Circular Lists

In a one-way grounded list, the pointer in the last dynamic record is null. To make a one-way grounded list into a one-way circular list, the pointer in the last record is set to point to the first record in the list. At first, it might appear that little if anything is gained by doing this, but this does turn out to be a very useful structure. In fact, this structure efficiently represents queues. The pointer to the circular list actually points to the record that contains the data for the last item in the queue. The pointer in that record points to the record that contains the first item in the queue. The pointers in the other records that form the queue link the records together, in front to rear order.

Since the list pointer, Q, points to the rear of the list, the enqueue operation, ENQ, is very direct. ENQ must handle the special condition of ENQing

```
1    PROGRAM queues (input, output);
2
3    TYPE
4       link = ↑qrec;
5       qrec = RECORD
6                  point : link;
7                  data : integer
8              END;
9
10   PROCEDURE enq (  VAR q: link;
11                   item : integer );
12
13       VAR
14          rear : link;
15
16       BEGIN
17       new (rear);  rear↑.data := item;
18       IF q = NIL THEN
19           rear↑.point := rear
20       ELSE
21           BEGIN
22           rear↑.point := q↑.point;
23           q↑.point := rear
24           END;
25        q := rear
26       END { of enq };
27
28   PROCEDURE deq ( VAR q : link;
29                   VAR item : integer );
30
31       VAR
32          front : link;
33
34       BEGIN
35       IF q = NIL THEN
36           writeln (' ATTEMPT TO DEQUEUE AN EMPTY QUEUE')
37       ELSE
38           BEGIN
39           front := q↑.point;   item := front↑.data;
40           IF q = front THEN
41               q := NIL
42           ELSE
43               q↑.point := front↑.point;
44           dispose (front)
45           END
46       END { of deq };
```

Figure 6.6. ENQ and DEQ algorithms for a queue in a circular list

onto an empty list. The dequeue algorithm, DEQ, must follow the pointer in the first record, which represents the end of the queue, to get to the record that is being dequeued. The DEQ algorithm must handle two special conditions, an empty queue and the case when the queue is about to become empty. Both algorithms function within a constant amount of time, and therefore are time efficient.

```
1     PROGRAM circulartsil ( input, output );
2
3     TYPE
4         pointer = ↑listrec;
5         listrec = RECORD
6                       link: pointer;
7                       data: integer
8                   END;
9
10    PROCEDURE tsil ( list: pointer );
11
12        VAR
13            prev, after, start: pointer;
14
15        BEGIN
16        prev := list;   start := list↑.link;   after := start↑.link;
17        WHILE list <> start DO
18            BEGIN
19            start↑.link := prev;
20            prev := start;
21            start := after;
22            after := after↑.link
23            END;
24        start↑.link := prev
25        END { of circular tsil };
```

Figure 6.7.   TSIL procedure for circular lists

Manipulating circular lists is not more complex than handling grounded lists. The distinction is that with a grounded list, a test for null indicates when the list has been traversed. In a circular list, a comparison between the pointer traversing the list and the original list pointer succeeds when the list is traversed. To see this, consider figure 6.7 which contains a TSIL algorithm for circular lists. Compare this algorithm to the TSIL algorithm for a grounded list. The only difference is in the terminating condition for the loop and the extra linking after the loop which makes the list circular. The similarities are emphasized even more with an exercise problem, namely, write one TSIL algorithm which handles both types of lists.

Circular lists can be used to represent both queues and stacks (see exercises). But, like one-way grounded lists, one-way circular lists have the same limitations that are forced on them by the one-way nature of their linking. However, one very obvious benefit to this dynamic allocation approach over the array wraparound approach of representing queues is that the bumping problem has disappeared along with any timing difficulties that were associated with handling bumping. But bumping has been eliminated at the cost of space, specifically the space required to store the pointers that link the lists and yield the logical structure.

6:3. Two-Way Linked Lists

The limitations due to the one-way nature of the sequential access in ground and circular lists can be eliminated by using two pointers in every dynamic record. The first pointer, as before, points to the next record in the list. The second pointer can be used to point to the previous record in the list. Figure 6.8 illustrates this. This adds an additional space cost of one pointer location per dynamic record, but for this cost, the ability to sequentially access in both directions is achieved. Every time a two-way linked record is inserted or deleted, the relinking costs are doubled. But if the relinking costs were originally bound by a constant, doubling that, hopefully, small constant amount of time, is still a reasonable cost, especially if the ability to access in both directions from a record is required.

There is one type of structure which two-way linked lists conveniently represent. The structure type is the double ended queue, dequeue, structure. They can be conveniently represented by circular two-way lists. An exercise problem describes algorithms to implement double ended queues.

6:4. EXERCISES

1. Write one piece of code that does the TSIL in O(size of list) time on both grounded and circular lists.

2. Write PUSH and POP to handle stacks in one-way circular lists. Which routines are identical, PUSH and ENQ, or, POP and DEQ? Are you sure?

3. Rewrite the quicksort algorithm using a dynamically allocated list to represent a pushdown stack with the two pointers that indicate the extent of the piece to be sorted stored together in one dynamically allocated record.

4. Write procedures to do the following manipulations with one-way ground lists:

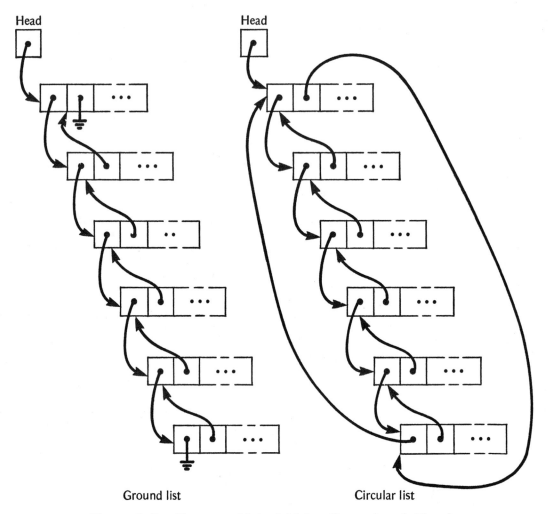

Figure 6.8. Two-way Linked Lists, Ground and Circular

a. FIND(ITEM, LIST) - Return the pointer to the first record in LIST
    containing ITEM, else return a null pointer;
b. INSERT(NEWREC, K, LIST) - Insert the record indicated by NEWREC
    after the K-th record in LIST, if K=0, NEWREC is made the first re-
    cord in the list (Be careful, especially in handling the case when
    K=0);

     c.   DELETE(ITEM, LIST) - Delete the first record in LIST that contains ITEM.

5.   Write the routines in exercise 4 for a two-way ground list. Describe the additional difficulties encountered in doing this.

6.   Write the routines in exercise 4 for a circular list. Compare the difficulties in writing these routines to the problems encountered in exercises 4 and 5.

7.   A double ended queue is a sequential structure where items can be inserted and deleted from either end and once items are placed in the structure, their relative positions remain the same. Write routines to implement a double ended queue as a two-way circular list. Write routines DQL, DQR, NQL, NQR, where the prefix "D" means dequeue, the prefix "N" means enqueue, the suffix "R" means the right end, and the suffix "L" means the left end. Also, an empty queue is indicated by a null list pointer.

8.   Describe the problems encountered when one-way grounded lists are used to represent queues.

9.   If p bits are used to store pointers and d bits are needed for each data item, what is the percentage of storage utilization for lists?

10. Rewrite the pointersort of figure 5.2 so that two lists are created. Each list should contain about half of the data in sorted order. Now, write a procedure MERGE (INTO, FROM1, FROM2) which accepts the two pointers FROM1 and FROM2 that point to the two sorted lists and creates a new list pointed to by INTO. This new list should be the merging of the two other lists into one fully sorted list of all the data.

7

Trees

Trees were introduced in 3:4. The value and power of trees, as a data structure, should become apparent, especially as one looks at the cost of representing them relative to the capabilities they provide. Several types of representations are described, from the simple use of arrays for some representations of binary trees to several methods that use pointers.

7:1. Binary Trees - Array Representation

A binary tree is a tree in which each node has at most two children. Intuitively, a binary tree is balanced if each node has exactly two children or no children and all the terminal nodes are at the same level. When a binary tree is almost balanced, and the items that are kept at the nodes of the tree are all the same type, then there is a straightforward way of representing the binary tree in an array. Refer to the two child nodes of each node as the left child and the right child and assume there is some way of distinguishing the two children of every node, then the tree can be stored in an array, call it TREE, as follows:

1. The root node is stored in the first location of the array, TREE(1);
2. For the node stored at position TREE(J), store its left child at TREE(2*J);
3. For the node stored at position TREE(J), store its right child at TREE(2*J+1).

Figure 7.1 illustrates the association between the nodes in a tree and their locations in the array. With this representation, given the index to a node, J, its children are at positions 2*J and 2*J+1, while its parent node is at

$$INT(J/2)$$

where INT is the function which gives the integer part of the division.

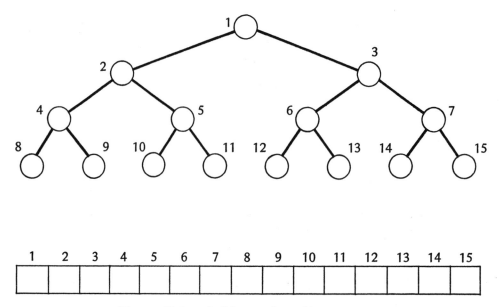

Figure 7.1. A Binary tree in an array

As long as the array is balanced, or close to it, the space in the array is used efficiently. If a node in the tree is a terminal node, then all the positions in the array which would hold descendents would be empty. For example, if the root node had only one child, then about half the space in the array would not be used. If one of the children of the root node has only one child, then only about 1/4 of the array is used. Exercise 7.1 illustrates a use of a tree which is not balanced, however the "wasted" space is more than compensated for by the improved efficiency over other methods of solving the problem.

An example of a use of a binary tree in an array is one of several sort techniques that are similar in structure. These techniques are called Heapsorts or Treesorts. They begin by viewing an unordered array of numbers as a tree, see figure 7.2. The array is sorted by using two processes. In process one, the tree is organized so that each parent is larger than both its children. This is referred to as a partial ordering, which will be described below. This could be done by the following algorithm: For each node, other than the root node, compare it to its parent. If the parent is larger, go on to the next node, otherwise, switch the node with its parent, back up, and continue to compare and switch either until the parent is larger, or until the

1	2	3	4	5	6	7	8	9	10	11	12	13	14	15
45	83	7	61	12	99	44	77	14	29	60	19	32	41	58

(a)   An unordered array

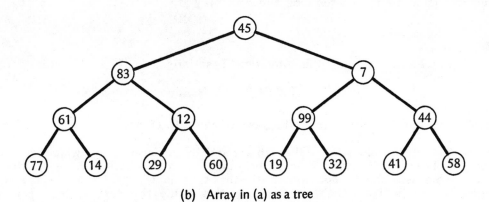

(b)   Array in (a) as a tree

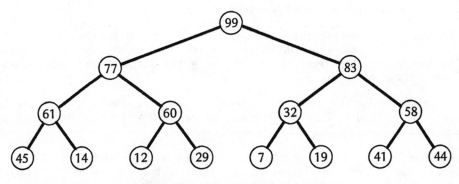

(c)   Tree after partial ordering

1	2	3	4	5	6	7	8	9	10	11	12	13	14	15
99	77	83	61	60	32	58	45	14	12	29	7	19	41	44

(d)   The tree of part (c) in an array

Figure 7.2.   Putting a heap in partial order

number is placed in the root position. Figure 7.2c illustrates the result of this operation on 7.2b. When 7.2c is written as an array, 7.2d, observe that the numbers are not in sorted order. This is why this is referred to as a partial ordering. As a matter of fact, the numbers appear to be close to reverse collating order, high to low.

What was the time cost of doing this partial ordering operation? Observe that, at most, each number could be moved from its position in the tree to the root of the tree. For a balanced binary tree with N nodes, the length of the longest path to the root, and hence the maximum number of times that a number would be moved towards the root, is

$$\log_2 N \ .$$

With N nodes in the tree, the total time T satisfies,

$$T < N * \log_2 N \ .$$

If close to partial order, then the time is close to O(N).

Phase two of the algorithm takes this partially ordered tree, which is in reverse collating order, and places the numbers into collating order in the array. This is done as follows, until the tree is empty: Remove the lower right most node from the tree and call this value the test value. Take the root node and place it in the array that is being used to hold the tree at the position vacated by the test value, see figure 7.3. Do the following until the test value is placed back into the tree.

> Compare the largest child of the vacant position in the tree to the test value, if the test value is larger, or no child exists, place the test value at the vacant position, otherwise move the largest child up to create a new vacant position.

These actions take the tree in figure 7.3a and transform it into the tree in figure 7.3b. Figure 7.3c illustrates the results after two iterations of this procedure.

A maximum bound can be established for the second phase of the heapsort. Observe that if the tree had N nodes, then N times a value is removed from the tree and placed at the position in the array that was vacated by the test value. The worst case for the placement of the test value back into the tree occurs when the test value is placed at a terminal node, that means log N loop iterations occur. So the time for the procedure is at most N * log N. Putting this together with the results for the first phase, the total time is bound by

$$O(2*n*\log_2 n \ ).$$

The entire two phase procedure can be performed in one array and several extra memory locations. Some details of keeping track of the status of phase two can be worked out as an exercise (Exercise 7.2).

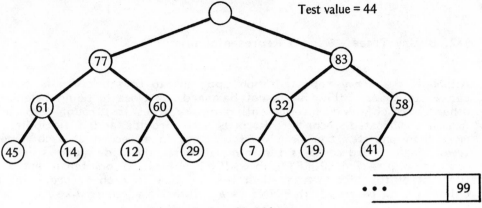

(a) Beginning of bubble-up

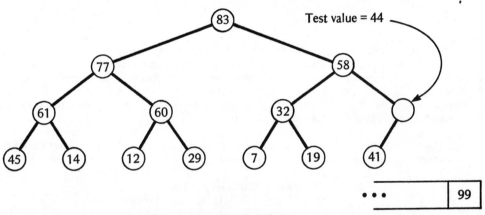

(b) Result after bubble-up

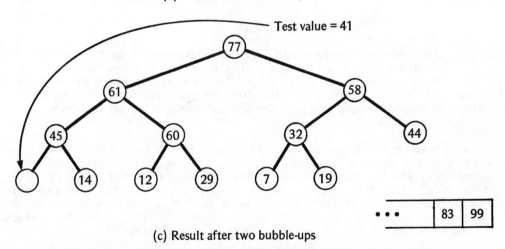

(c) Result after two bubble-ups

Figure 7.3. Result of part two of the heapsort procedure

7:2. Binary Trees - Record Representation

Although the array representation approach to binary trees is powerful, it can waste space if the tree is not balanced, or close to being balanced. Another approach towards representing binary trees is through the use of dynamically allocated records. Records also provide added flexibility in that more than one item can be stored together in a record at each node in the tree. Each record contains the information for the node along with two pointers, see figure 7.4, PLEFT and PRIGHT. First, a pointer is established to the root of the binary tree, then the pointers in each record point to their children node records. If POINT is a pointer to a record like

```
treerec = RECORD
            pleft  : ↑treerec;
            pright : ↑treerec;
                       . . .
          END;
```

then POINT↑.PLEFT points to the left child of the node and POINT↑.PRIGHT points to the right child. With this pointer approach, the tree structure can be easily traversed using an auxiliary structure, a queue, stack, etc. That is, if one pointer is followed from a node, the other pointer can be saved so that the other subtree of the node can eventually be accessed. This is discussed further in section 7:4.

Another method of linking a binary tree is to use three pointers per record, a left child pointer, a right child pointer, and a parent pointer, as in

```
tree = RECORD
         leftch  : ↑tree;
         rightch : ↑tree;
         parent  : ↑tree;
                    . . .
       END;
```

With this approach, each child has immediate access to its parent. However, this is gained at a space cost of one extra memory location per record. Whether this cost is worth it has to be measured against the application. As you will see in section 7:4, the three pointer approach can be used to perform a natural order tree search without the use of an auxiliary structure, a pushdown stack.

In comparing these two approaches, recall that a tree was originally presented as a special type of graph or digraph. In the first representation, with two pointers, the digraph is evident in the direction of the pointers, from parent to child. The three pointer approach gives a bidirectionality between parent and child in that it is relatively easy to follow pointers in either direction, from the parent to the child, or vice versa. In either case, there is no wasted space in the sense that records are dynamically allocated only when nodes exist whereas in the array representation of a binary tree, array space could be allocated but unused if the node did not exist. Examples of the uses of these allocation methods are described in the following section.

7:3. General Tree Representations

At first, after seeing these ways of representing binary trees, one might attempt to generalize from these approaches. For example, by multiplying and dividing by 2, a binary tree could be allocated in an array. By using two pointers per record, a binary tree could be allocated using dynamic records. One might begin by considering using 3 pointers per record for a ternary tree, or multiplying and dividing by 3 for an array representation of a ternary tree. However, there are several pitfalls that one might encounter.

Consider representing a ternary tree in an array. The root must be at location 1 in the array. Its children are at locations 2, 3, and 4, and these indices must be computed in a formula which multiplies by 3, that is, 3*1-1, 3*1, and 3*1+1. The children of the node at location 2 must be at locations 5, 6, and 7. This is 3*2-1, 3*2, and 3*2+1. Generalizing this yields the formula for the indices of the children of a node at position I as

$$3*J-1, \ 3*J, \ \text{AND} \ 3*J+1,$$

and the parent of the node at position J has index

$$\text{INT} \ (\ (J+1)/3 \ ).$$

Observe that the formula for calculating the parent required some adjustment of the index J before the division. Generalizing this to an n-ary tree is given as an exercise. One should observe that the same space problems occur with n-ary trees as occur with binary trees allocated in an array. That is, if the tree is not close to being balanced, the amount of unused space in the array can be quite large. Also, the formula for index calculations for the location of child and parent nodes in ternary and n-ary trees, although they are fairly simple, they require a little more thought when you use them as compared to the index calculation formulas for the binary tree representation in an array.

Generalizing the record approach for binary trees to n-ary trees creates other kinds of problems. Specifically, for an n-ary tree, if n pointers are going to appear in each record, if the node has substantially fewer than n children, a good amount of space could be wasted keeping null pointers. Also, writing general routines that automatically handle n-ary trees, for any value n, could be difficult.

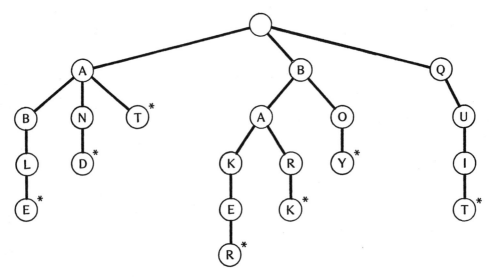

Figure 7.4.   Storing words in an n-ary Tree

Fortunately, there is an approach which is convenient in terms of space allocation and it handles n-ary trees for all n. This approach uses two pointers per record like in the binary tree case. However, this time, the children node of each node are thought of as being organized from left to right below the parent, see figure 7.4. Then, rather than using a LEFTCH and RIGHTCH pointer as in the binary case, what used to be the left child pointer is now the pointer to the leftmost child. Rather than having a right child pointer, the second pointer is a sibling pointer, that is, each node contains a pointer to the sibling node (node with the same parent) that is immediately to its right,

```
tree = RECORD
            child   : ↑tree;
            sibling : ↑tree;
                  . . .
        END;
```

This is illustrated for figure 7.4 in figure 7.5.

Algorithms to create trees in this form and manipulate the information in these trees are surprisingly simple. To illustrate this, consider a tree structure that contains words in a dictionary. Specifically, suppose it is desired to have a tree containing the list of words,

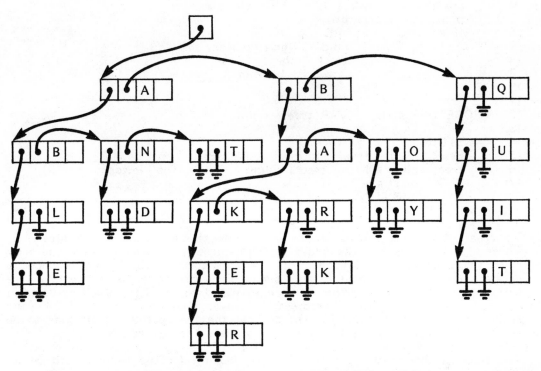

Figure 7.5.   Record representation of figure 7.4

able
baker
boy
bark
and
at
quit

The tree in figure 7.4 contains these words in that starting at the root node, by tracing down the tree to any marked node, yields one of these words. This tree does not contain the word "an" because the "n" node is not marked. This tree is in alphabetic order in that if the path associated to one word is to the left of the path associated to another word, then the first word comes before the second in alphabetic order. Figure 7.5 illustrates a record representation of this tree.

```
1     PROGRAM treestartup (input, output);
2
3     TYPE
4         anarray = ARRAY [ 1..50 ] OF char;
5         pointer = ↑treerecord;
6         treerecord = RECORD
7                             child, sibling:pointer;
8                             letter : char;
9                             endword: boolean;
10                        END;
11
12    PROCEDURE strtre ( VAR tree : pointer );
13
14        BEGIN
15        new( tree );  tree↑.endword := FALSE;
16        tree↑.child := NIL;  tree↑.sibling := NIL;  tree↑.letter := chr(0)
17        END { of strtre };
18                { CONTINUED ON THE NEXT PAGE }
```

To create this tree representation, consider the algorithms in figure 7.6. These algorithms assume the codes for alphanumeric characters have the same collating order as the alphabet. The first algorithm, STRTRE, is used to create a tree. The purpose of this simple little procedure is to create a tree with one record in it. Further, this one record contains the smallest value in the collating order of the characters, whatever that happens to be for your computer. This procedure guarantees that the tree pointer never has to be reset. That simplifies the tree building process (see exercises).

The BLDTRE algorithm traverses the tree looking for the letters in the word. At level i, a search is made through the tree for the letter in **word** [i]. The SIBLING pointer is followed across until the letter is found, it is determined that the letter is not in this level, or a null SIBLING pointer is encountered. If it is in the tree, the CHILD pointer is followed down to the next level. If the letter is not there, GETREC is called and the letter is appropriately placed into the tree. Note that there were two ways of determining if the letter was not in the tree, either by a comparison to the next letter, or a null SIBLING pointer. In either case, the new record is inserted so that the SIBLING pointers maintain the collating order.

Figure 7.7 illustrates the STRTRE and BLDTRE algorithms for trees kept as dynamic records with three pointers, CHILD, SIBLING, and PARENT. Note that from the form and size of the algorithms, they are not more complex in that there is more looping or conditional structure than the two-pointer versions. Figure 7.8 illustrates a way of visualizing the use of three pointers. As in the two pointer linking, there are "child" and "sibling" pointers. With three pointers, the third pointer is used to locate the "parent" record of each record. A use of a three-pointer approach is described below in section 7:4. Obviously, the three pointer approach has the added cost of a pointer per record. This cost must be weighed in light of the space cost versus computer time or programming time for a particular application.

```
19    PROCEDURE bldtre ( VAR tree : pointer;
20                          word : anarray;
21                          size : integer );
22
23       VAR
24          anew, prev, this : pointer;
25          lastdisp, i : integer;
26
27       BEGIN
28       i := 1;   this := tree;
29       WHILE i <= size DO
30          IF ( this = NIL ) OR ( this↑.letter > word[i] ) THEN
31             BEGIN
32             new( anew );   anew↑.letter := word[i];
33             anew↑.sibling := this;   anew↑.endword := FALSE;
34             IF lastdisp = 1 THEN
35                 prev↑.child := anew
36             ELSE
37                 prev↑.sibling := anew;
38             lastdisp := 1;   prev := anew;   this := NIL;
39             i := i + 1    END
40          ELSE
41             IF this↑.letter = word[i] THEN
42                 BEGIN
43                 prev := this;   lastdisp := 1;
44                 i := i + 1;   this := prev↑.child
45                 END
46             ELSE
47                 BEGIN
48                 prev := this;   lastdisp := 2;   this := this↑.sibling
49                 END
50       END { of bldtre };
```

Figure 7.6.   Starttree and buildtree procedures

7:4. Tree Searching

There are many ways that one might wish to search through a tree to find information.   However, two classical search patterns are referred to as a level-
by-level tree search and a natural ordered tree search.   In a level-by-level
tree search, it is desired to go across the tree from node to node, a level at
a time.   In a natural order tree search, the search begins by going down
the left most child of each node until a terminal node is encountered.   From
this point, it is desirable always to seek out the left most terminal node that
can be achieved from any particular node.   The process then retraces its
steps until a next left most sibling is found, then from that sibling the
search is made for the left most terminal node in its subtree.   Although these
two search techniques appear to be so different, see figures 7.9 and 7.10,
the algorithmic structures used to perform them are surprisingly similar.

```
1     PROGRAM treestartup (input, output);
2
3     TYPE
4         anarray = ARRAY [ 1..50 ] OF char;
5         pointer = ↑treerecord;
6         treerecord = RECORD
7                         child, sibling, parent : pointer;
8                         letter : char;
9                         endword: boolean;
10                    END;
11
12    PROCEDURE strtre ( VAR tree : pointer );
13
14        BEGIN
15        new( tree );
16        tree↑.child := NIL;   tree↑.sibling := NIL;
17        tree↑.parent := NIL;   tree↑.letter := chr(0)
18        END { of strtre };
19              { CONTINUED ON THE NEXT PAGE }
```

Figure 7.11 illustrates a level-by-level tree search algorithm. If a tree is dynamically allocated using two pointers, the level-by-level search is accomplished by following the SIBLING pointers, as long as they are not null and enqueuing the CHILD pointers. Obviously, following the SIBLING pointers takes the search along a level under a particular node. Then, since the CHILD pointers are enqueued, the first child pointer in the queue is the left most child of the left most node at the previous level. Therefore, by enqueuing the CHILD pointers the information is kept in first in, first out order and the search proceeds a level at a time.

If a level-by-level tree search algorithm is described as basically enqueuing the CHILD pointer and following the SIBLING pointer, then a natural order tree search is described as PUSHING the SIBLING pointer and following the CHILD pointer. By making these changes in the level-by-level tree search algorithm, that is, use PUSH and POP rather than ENQ and DEQ along with which pointer is saved and which is followed, a natural order tree search results.

One example of the use of a natural order tree search is with a dictionary tree. Suppose it is desirable to have a procedure that lists the words in the tree in alphabetical order. As each node is processed by the natural order tree search, the character that is in the node's record is copied onto the end of the character string. When the procedure backs up, that is, each time the pushdown stack is popped, the last character is removed from the end of the string. Every time a "marked" node is encountered, that is, a node that indicates the end of a word, printing this string of characters, will print the word. Therefore, if this is done in conjunction with a natural order tree search, the words in the dictionary tree are printed in alphabetic order. Keeping the array of letters for printing can be done as follows:

```
20    PROCEDURE bldtre ( VAR tree : pointer;
21                         word : anarray;
22                         size : integer );
23
24       VAR
25          anew, prev, this, ancestor : pointer;
26          lastdisp, i : integer;
27
28       BEGIN
29       i := 1;  this := tree;  ancestor := NIL;
30       WHILE i <= size DO
31          IF ( this = NIL ) OR ( this↑.letter > word[i] ) THEN
32             BEGIN
33             new( anew );  anew↑.letter := word[i];
34             anew↑.sibling := this;  new↑.parent := ancestor;
35             IF lastdisp = 1 THEN
36                prev↑.child := anew
37             ELSE
38                prev↑.sibling := anew;
39             lastdisp := 1;  prev := anew;  this := NIL;
40             ancestor := prev;  i := i + 1    END
41          ELSE
42             IF this↑.letter = word[i] THEN
43                BEGIN
44                prev := this;  lastdisp := 1;
45                i := i + 1;  this := prev↑.child;  ancestor := prev
46                END
47             ELSE
48                BEGIN
49                prev := this;  lastdisp := 2;  this := this↑.sibling
50                END
51       END { of bldtre };
```

Figure 7.7. Three pointer versions of Starttree and Buildtree

1. Keep an index J into the array, this index also keeps the depth of the tree search;
2. Every time a node is encountered, add 1 to J and use J as an index in storing the letter in the LETTER array;
3. Every time a NULL pointer is encountered, subtract 1 from J.

The three pointer approach to representing a tree lends itself to a natural order tree search. This can be accomplished without a pushdown stack because the PARENT pointers provide a way for working backwards up a tree without having to store information in a stack. Figure 7.12 illustrates an algorithm for performing a natural order tree search on a three pointer tree structure. The algorithm proceeds, as in the case with a pushdown stack, by simply following the CHILD pointers to the left most terminal node. Once a NULL CHILD pointer is encountered, the PARENT pointers are used to

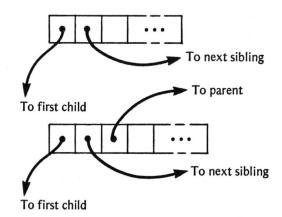

Figure 7.8.   Abstraction of three pointer records

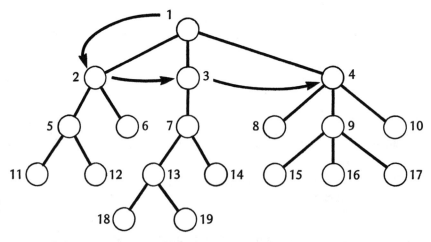

Figure 7.9.   Sequence of Nodes in a Level-by-Level Tree Search

backtrack up the tree until a non-NULL SIBLING pointer is found. At this point, the SIBLING pointer is followed and the algorithm once again proceeds by following CHILD pointers.

It is worthwhile to compare the timings of the two natural order tree search algorithms. The natural order tree search algorithm that uses a pushdown

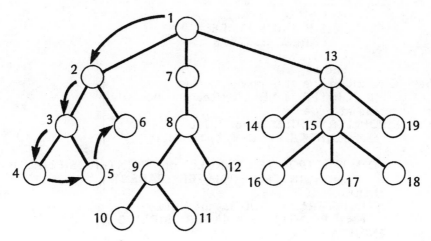

Figure 7.10.   Sequence of Nodes in a Natural Order Tree Search

```
 1:   tree : RECORD
 2:              child : ↑tree;
 3:              sibling : ↑tree
 4:                  . . .
 5:          END;
 6:   ENQ the tree pointer into the Queue
 7:   Set POINTER to NIL
 8:   DO UNTIL (  (the queue is empty and the POINTER is NIL )  or
 9:   :              until the search succeeds)
10:   :    IF the POINTER is NIL
11:   :        DEQ a POINTER from the queue
12:   :    ENDIF
13:   :    IF the POINTER is not NIL
14:   :        perform whatever work that is to be accomplished
15:   :              with the node indicated by this POINTER
16:   :        ENQ the CHILD pointer (POINTER↑.CHILD) from this node
17:   :        reset the pointer to the SIBLING pointer (POINTER↑.SIBLING)
18:   :    ENDIF
19:   ENDDO
```

Figure 7.11.   Level-by-level Algorithm

stack has the same structure as the level-by-level tree search. A quick look
at its structure indicates that there is one loop iteration for each node in the
tree, and one loop iteration every time POINTER becomes null, that is, every
time a node had a null CHILD or SIBLING pointer. This produces a timing of

```
 1:   type
 2:       TREE : Record
 3:                   CHILD : ↑TREE;
 4:                   SIBLING : ↑TREE;
 5:                   PARENT : ↑TREE;
 6:                       . . .
 7:               end;
 8:   Set POINTER to the tree pointer value
 9:   DO UNTIL POINTER is NULL or search succeeds
10:   :   process at node
11:   :   IF POINTER↑.CHILD is not NULL
12:   :       reset POINTER to POINTER↑.CHILD
13:   :   ELSE
14:   :       DO UNTIL (POINTER is NULL) or (POINTER↑.SIBLING is not NULL)
15:   :       :   reset POINTER to POINTER↑.PARENT
16:   :       ENDDO
17:   :       IF POINTER↑.SIBLING is not NULL
18:   :           reset POINTER to POINTER↑.SIBLING
18:   :       ENDIF
20:   :   ENDIF
21:   ENDDO
```

Figure 7.12.   Natural Order Tree Search Without a Stack

O (NO. of nodes + NO. of null pointers in nodes) .

For the three pointer algorithm, there is one iteration of the outer loop for every non-null CHILD pointer. The inner loop backs up the tree until it finds a non-null SIBLING pointer. In general, it cannot be determined how many CHILD pointers and how many SIBLING pointers exist, except that both of these numbers are bound by the number of nodes in the tree. Therefore, the second algorithm is bound by

O (2* No. of nodes) .

Since the number of null pointers in a tree is also bound by the number of nodes in the tree, both of these algorithms function in the same order of magnitude of time. Can a natural order tree search be done without a push-down stack and without a PARENT pointer? The answer is yes, but! Assume there is extra space in each record,

```
            tree = RECORD
                        child : ↑tree;
                        sibling : ↑tree;
                            . . .
            END;
```

```
 1:   type
 2:          TREE: record
 3:                  CHILD : ↑TREE;
 4:                  SIBLING : ↑TREE;
 5:                  PARENT : ↑TREE;
 6:                  MARK : BOOLEAN;
 7:                        . . .
 8:             end;
 9:   DO until search succeeds or ROOT↑.MARK is TRUE
10:  :   set POINTER to ROOT
11:  :   DO UNTIL POINTER↑.MARK is TRUE or search succeeds
12:  :   :   perform your search process on the node here
13:  :   :   IF POINTER↑.CHILD is not NULL
     :   :              and POINTER↑.CHILD↑.MARK is FALSE
14:  :   :      reset POINTER to POINTER↑.CHILD
15:  :   :   ELSEIF POINTER↑.SIBLING is not null and
16:  :   :                 and POINTER↑.SIBLING↑.MARK is FALSE
17:  :   :      reset POINTER to POINTER↑.SIBLING
18:  :   :   ELSE
19:  :   :      set POINTER↑.MARK to true
20:  :   :   ENDIF
21:  :   ENDDO
22:   ENDDO
```

Figure 7.13. Natural order tree search without a stack or third pointer

This extra space need only be one bit or boolean variable called MARK. Further, assume that these bits are all set to indicate a false boolean value. Now, consider the algorithm in figure 7.13. This search does a natural order tree search until it hits a marked node. Then, it tries to go around the marked node by following a SIBLING pointer. When it cannot go down the tree any further, it marks the node it is pointing to. This search takes a long time. Each time a node is marked, it searches a path. Therefore, the time to mark a node is bound by the length of the longest path in the tree, which in turn is bound by the number of nodes in the tree. Therefore, the time to search the tree is,

$$O (N*L) \leq O (N^2),$$

where N is the number of nodes and L is the length of the longest path.

Although recursion is not formally introduced until chapter 11, the natural order tree search algorithm lends itself so well to the introduction of that topic, that we include figure 7.14 which illustrates a recursive natural order tree search. For those who wish to learn more about recursion at this point, we suggest that you proceed to chapter 11, then return to this point after completing chapter 11. If root is the name of the pointer to the root of the tree, then the procedure in figure 7.14 is called with root as its argument, **natural (root)**.

```
 1  PROGRAM recursivenaturalordertreesearch (input, output)
 2
 3  TYPE
 4     tpoint = ↑treerecord;
 5     treerecord = RECORD
 6                     child, sibling: tpoint;
 7                     ... other items in record ...
 8                  END;
 9
10  PROCEDURE natural (node: tpoint);
11
12     BEGIN
13     IF node↑.child <> NIL
14       THEN natural (node↑.child);
15
16     { code to process the node goes here }
17
18     IF node↑.sibling <> NIL
19       THEN natural (node↑.sibling)
20     END
```

Figure 7.14.   Recursive natural order tree search.

7:5. EXERCISES

1. Morse Code Revisited - Store the letter and numerals in an array as a binary tree using the following scheme:

   a.   Leave the root empty;
   b.   To store a letter in the tree, use its Morse Code as follows: Starting with an index of 1, scan the Morse Code of the letter from left to right, each time a dot is encountered, multiply the index by two each time a dash is encountered, multiply the index by two then add one, After the Morse code is scanned, use the computed index to store the letter in the array.

   Note that "." means left child and "-" means right child. Now encode messages in Morse Code using "/" to separate the codes for letters and "//" to separate words, for example,

                                    a cat

   would be encoded as

                           .-//-.-./.-/-//   .

Write a program which decodes messages in this way. Evaluate the time and space requirements of this approach relative to the table look-up translation scheme presented in chapter 1. What variable(s) control the time it takes to decode the message using trees? What variables(s) control the time it takes to decode the message using a table look-up? To what extent does the use of a binary tree improve the speed of the decoding process?

```
A.-        J.---      S...       2..---
B-...      K-.-       T-         3...--
C-.-.      L.--       U..-       4....-
D-..       M--        V...-      5.....
E.         N-.        W.--       6-....
F..-.      O---       X-..-      7--...
G--.       P.--.      Y-.--      8---..
H....      Q--.-      Z--..      9----.
I..        R.-.       1.----     0-----
```

Figure 7.15.   International Morse Code

2. Carry out the two procedures to perform the heapsort. Place counters in your code and compare the actual number of loop iterations you obtain to the bound described in the text. Also, what results are obtained for various special cases (numbers in order, numbers in reverse order).

3. Write the procedures to create, build, and find words in a dictionary tree.

4. Write a procedure to do a natural order tree search through a dictionary tree and print the words in the dictionary in alphabetic order.

5. Investigate the problems encountered when a STRTREE routine is replaced by simply starting with a null pointer to indicate an empty tree.

6. Write a single procedure which does the work of both the build and the find procedures for a dictionary tree.

7. Derive the general formula for allocating an n-ary tree in an array.

8. Write a pseudocode representation of the natural order tree search algorithm.

9. Write an algorithm to print the words in a dictionary tree in alphabetical order.

8

Graphs, Digraphs, and More Trees

Just as trees can be represented in various ways, so can graphs and digraphs. Starting with simple matrix representations of graphs to a variety of linked approaches, the problems are compounded by the fact that graphs and digraphs are used along with other structures like trees, queues, and stacks. Often, that auxiliary structure is a tree and as the tree is being constructed, it must be searched.

Besides introducing methods of representing graphs and digraphs, this section gives several examples of tree searching in action. Also, included in this section is a tree balancing algorithm. Justifications for this algorithm and its timing are easy to come by. Although it is relatively easy to understand conceptually how the algorithm works, there are a lot of details that must be kept in order. For this reason, one must carefully observe those details when constructing an AVL tree rebalancing algorithm.

8:1. Elementary Digraph and Graph Representations

Recall, a digraph is an ordered pair, (V,A). The first set, V, is the set of vertices. The second, A, is a collection of ordered pairs of vertices, called arcs. A digraph can be easily represented in matrix form, see figure 8.1 and its representation in 8.2, such that if the digraph has n vertices, then it can be represented in an n by n matrix as follows:

a. Number the vertices 1 through n;
b. An arc from node i to node j is represented in the matrix by

$$a_{ij} = 1,$$

otherwise,

$$a_{ij} = 0.$$

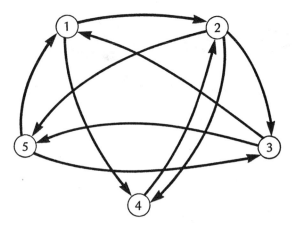

Figure 8.1. A Digraph

With this approach, digraph problems can be solved using operations that are similar to matrix multiplication. For example, the connection matrix tells us directly which nodes are connected to others with a single arc. If A is the connection matrix for a graph, and

$$A^N$$

is the matrix multiplication of A with itself N times. Define

$$A'^N$$

such that

$$a'_{ij} = 1 \text{ if and only if } a_{ij} \neq 0,$$

otherwise $a_{ij} = 0$. That is, perform the matrix multiplication and set all non-zero values in the result to one. Then

$$A'^N$$

describes the nodes that are connected by a path of length N.

To see this, consider the matrix multiplication AxA of the matrix in figure 8.2. If B = AxA, then

$$b_{ij} = a_{i1}*a_{1j} + a_{i2}*a_{2j} + \ldots + a_{in}*a_{nj} \quad .$$

That is,

$$b_{ij} \neq 0$$

$$
\begin{array}{c c}
 & \begin{array}{c c c c c} 1 & 2 & 3 & 4 & 5 \end{array} \\
\begin{array}{c} 1 \\ 2 \\ 3 \\ 4 \\ 5 \end{array} &
\left[\begin{array}{c c c c c}
0 & 1 & 0 & 1 & 0 \\
0 & 0 & 1 & 1 & 1 \\
1 & 0 & 0 & 0 & 1 \\
0 & 1 & 0 & 0 & 0 \\
1 & 0 & 1 & 0 & 0
\end{array} \right]
\end{array}
$$

Figure 8.2. Matrix representation of figure 8.1

if and only if there is some node k such that there is a path between nodes i to k and a path between nodes k and j. From this the relation between matrix multiplication and connectedness can be observed.

Consider the simple problem of determining if a digraph is connected. To do this, create a matrix A" from A as follows:

$$a''_{ij} = a_{ij} \text{ if } i \neq j \text{ and } a''_{ii} = 1 \text{ for all } i.$$

That is, make all the elements along the main diagonal of the connection matrix non-zero. Now, perform matrix multiplication on A". A", besides containing the information in A, also indicates that each node is connected to itself by a path of length 0 as well as a path of length 1. Then A"xA" indicates all nodes connected by paths of length 0, 1, and 2. In general,

$$A''^N$$

indicates all nodes connected with paths of length 0 through N. Therefore, if N > n, then

$$A''^N$$

indicates the connectedness of the digraph.

Since the arcs in a graph have no direction, a full matrix is not required. That is, the arc that connects node i to node j also connects node j to node i. One of two matrix approaches could be taken. The simplest perhaps would be to use the matrix, as in the case of digraphs, and store the information redundantly. That is, if there is an arc between nodes i and j, then in the matrix A,

$$a_{ij} = a_{ji} = 1.$$

By doing this, all the routines that find information about digraphs also work for graphs.

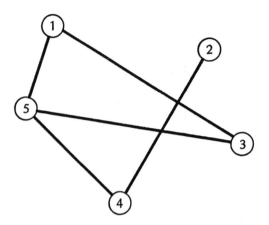

Figure 8.3.   A Graph

However, the matrix contains redundant information, about half the space in the matrix is wasted.   An alternate approach for graphs stores the arc information in a triangular matrix and uses the indexing manipulations that store a triangular matrix in an array (see 1:2).

$$
\begin{array}{cccccc}
1 & \begin{bmatrix} 0 \\ 0 & 0 \\ 1 & 0 & 0 \\ 0 & 1 & 0 & 0 \\ 1 & 0 & 1 & 1 & 0 \end{bmatrix} \\
\\
& 1 & 2 & 3 & 4 & 5
\end{array}
$$

Figure 8.4. Triangular matrix representation of figure 8.3

Figure 8.3 illustrates a graph and 8.4 is its triangular matrix representation. If B is the triangular matrix representation of a graph, then to determine if node i is connected to node j:

   a.   If i > j, then

$$b_{ij} = 1;$$

   b.   Otherwise,

$$b_{ji} = 1.$$

Routines can be written to perform the matrix-like multiplication on triangular forms that execute in the same order of time as the standard matrix multiplication procedures,

$$O(n^3),$$

or better. Further, one might assume that the triangular matrix form can be made more space efficient when used to represent graphs by eliminating the spaces

$$a_{ii} \text{ for all i.}$$

However, those spaces are required if the method used to form A" is applied to the triangular form to obtain the equivalent to the connection matrix.

In either case, an evaluation of the space utilization should be made. Consider the case where a matrix is used to store the connection information for a graphic representation of the map of the continental United States. There are 48 contiguous states, nodes, and no state is bounded by more than 8 other states. This means that fewer than 700 of the 2304 locations in the matrix are non-zero. That is, less than 1/3 of the space in the matrix is utilized. In reality, much less than 1/3 is utilized. As the number of nodes in the graph grows, the size of the matrix grows by $O(n*n)$, therefore, a considerable amount of space is used. In addition, to determine connectedness, the space required for the matrix is multiplied by two or three because several matrices are used to perform these matrix multiplication operations.

Also, one should not overlook the time required to determine the connectedness of the graph. Matrix multiplications require a large number of multiplications and additions to multiply an n by n matrix (see exercises).

8:2. Alternate Graph Representations

Rather than discussing methods for representing both graphs and digraphs we concentrate on methods for representing digraphs. These methods can be used to represent graphs just as the matrix approach was used to represent graphs by including redundant information in the representation. The justification for this is that although the information is stored redundantly, and hence, some space is wasted, this trades off favorably with human effort in that the procedures which manipulate digraphs also manipulate graphs. Hence, one set of procedures serve two purposes, one to manipulate graphs and one to manipulate digraphs.

$$
\begin{array}{c}
\begin{array}{ccc} 1 & 2 & 3 \end{array} \\
\begin{array}{c} 1 \\ 2 \\ 3 \\ 4 \\ 5 \end{array}
\begin{bmatrix}
2 & 4 & 0 \\
5 & 3 & 4 \\
1 & 5 & 0 \\
2 & 0 & 0 \\
1 & 3 & 0
\end{bmatrix}
\end{array}
\qquad
\begin{array}{c}
\begin{array}{c} 1 \\ 2 \\ 3 \\ 4 \\ 5 \\ 6 \\ 7 \\ 8 \\ 9 \\ 10 \end{array}
\begin{bmatrix}
1 & 2 \\
1 & 4 \\
2 & 5 \\
2 & 3 \\
2 & 4 \\
3 & 1 \\
3 & 5 \\
4 & 2 \\
5 & 1 \\
5 & 3
\end{bmatrix}
\end{array}
$$

(a) Node Path Table   (b)   Arc Incidence Table

Figure 8.5.   Table representations of the graph of figure 8.1

Two dimensional arrays can represent graphs. Here, there are two possible approaches. In one approach, the number of rows in the table equals the number of nodes in the graph. The number of columns in the table is greater than or at least equal to the maximum of the number of times any one node appears in an arc. For a graph of the contiguous United States, a 48x7 table would be sufficient. Figure 8.5a illustrates the node connection table for the graph in figure 8.1. This table is 60 percent of the size of the matrix representation of the graph. As the number of nodes in the graph increases but the number of arcs per node remains relatively constant, this approach does have a considerable space savings over the matrix approach. That is, for n nodes, if each node appears in at most k arcs, the size of the table is k*n while the matrix contains n*n locations. Since n > k, n*n > n*k.

Figure 8.5b illustrates another table oriented graph representation. In this approach a k by 2 table is used, where k is the number of arcs in the graph. Each row of the table lists a pair of nodes connected by an arc. Table 8.5b has 20 entries. This does not represent a great space savings over the matrix in figure 8.2. However, for a graph with n nodes and k arcs, the matrix representation has

$$O(\ n^2\ )$$

entries while the arc table has 2k entries.

Also, the arc table is more versatile. For example, suppose there are multiple arcs between two nodes and each arc must be labelled with some value. The entries in the matrix of 8.2 could indicate the count of the number of arcs between each pair of nodes or the value of the label on the arc, but not both (without using an encoding scheme which is beyond the scope of this text).

Relatively simple procedures can be created to work with table representations of graphs. Some of these are described in section 8:5. However, the table is not usually completely filled. Also, the number of columns in the table must be carefully specified so that it is large enough for the graph.

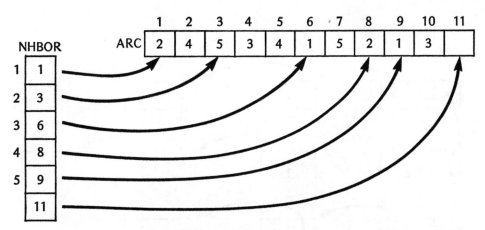

Figure 8.6.   A vector representation of the graph of figure 8.1

A third approach completely eliminates any wasted space inside of arrays. This approach, called a vector approach, is illustrated in figure 8.6. Here two vectors represent the digraph. The first vector, NHBOR, points to locations in the second vector, ARC, in such a way that all the neighbors of node J appear in locations ARC(NHBOR(J)) through ARC(NHBOR(J+1)-1). For a digraph with n nodes and a arcs, the NHBOR array must contain n+1 positions and ARC must have a positions.

8:3. Linked Representation

Dynamic allocation can also be used to represent a graph. One approach keeps the nodes of the graph in a linked list. From each record in the list, have a pointer to another linked list that contains the arc information of the node. Figure 8.7 illustrates a linked representation of the graph in figure 8.1. The dynamic allocation approach has an added advantage in that space can be provided in the dynamic records, both for nodes and for arcs, for any additional information about the node or arc that might be useful for the particular application of the graph.

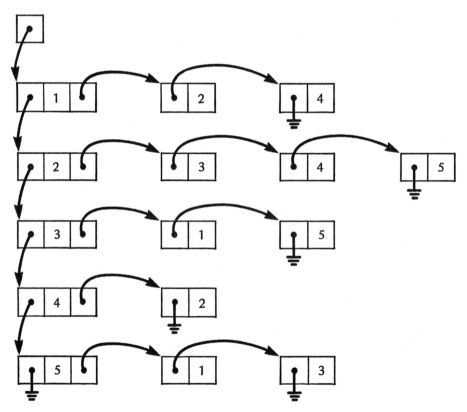

Figure 8.7. A linked representation of the graph of figure 8.1

Figure 8.8 illustrates a procedure which creates a linked representation of a graph. The assumption is that the nodes are numbered or indicated by some string of characters. The displacements NAME and ARCNAME can be any TYPE. They do not have to be strings of characters. Also, the procedure assumes that each "read" operation returns an ordered pair of data items, K and J, which are the same type as the displacements NAME and ARCNAME. The procedure reads the pairs, one at a time, finds the position in the NODE list of the node K, and places the node K in the list if it is not already there. Then the information about the arc from K to J is linked to the node record of the K node. There are two loops in the procedure, the main loop of the procedure, and within that, the loop in GETNODE. GETNODE executes each time the main procedure is called. If n is the number of nodes in the graph and k is the number of arcs, then the main loop executes k times. Each time it iterates, the loop in GETNODE iterates at most n times. Therefore the procedure executes in time bound by O(k*n).

It will become obvious in section 8:4 that the procedure in figure 8.7 does not quite put the representation of the graph into the right form. Specifically, rather than just having the ARCNAME in the ARCRECORDs, it would be much more convenient to have a pointer to the record that contained the node which is linked to the given node by this arc. That is, rather than having

```
TYPE
    arcrecord = RECORD
                    link : ↑arcrecord;
                    name : charstring
                END;
```

it would be more convenient to have

```
TYPE
    arcrecord = RECORD
                    link : ↑arcrecord;
                    arcto : ↑noderecord
                END.
```

Then procedures that use the linked representation would have pointers to the nodes in arc records rather than just the name or number of the node. By having a pointer to the node rather than just the name of the node the procedure can execute more quickly. If only the name of the node was known, the procedure would then have to spend time finding the node in the list of nodes. This would have to be done each time an arc is traversed and the accumulative effect on the procedure's timing could be disastrous.

```
1    PROGRAM linkedgraph (input, output, nodedata );
2
3    TYPE
4        charstring = PACKED ARRAY [1..8] OF char;
5        nodepoint = ↑noderecord;
6        arcpoint = ↑arcrecord;
7        noderecord = RECORD
8                         nodelink : nodepoint;
9                         name : charstring
10                        arclist : arcpoint
11                    END;
12       arcrecord = RECORD
13                       link : arcpoint;
14                       arcname : charstring
15                   END;
16
17   VAR
18       node, nodelist : nodepoint;
19       i, j : charstring;
20       nodedata : text;
21
22   PROCEDURE getpointer ( x : charstring;
23                          VAR point : nodepoint );
24
25       VAR
26          point : nodepoint;
27
28       BEGIN
29       point := nodelist;
30       WHILE ( point <> NIL ) AND ( point↑.name <> x ) DO
31           point := point↑.nodelink;
32       IF point = NIL THEN
33           BEGIN
34           new(point);  point↑.name := x;
35           point↑.nodelink := nodelist;  nodelist := point
36           END
37       END { of getpointer }
38           {  CONTINUED ON THE NEXT PAGE  }
```

8:4. Speed-up

Figure 8.9 illustrates a variation of the procedure in 8.8 which accomplishes
the desired result, namely, the ARCRECORDs contain pointers to the nodes
rather than just containing the names of the nodes.   This procedure's time
cost is more than the time cost of the procedure in 8.8 because of the extra
call to GETNODE in the main loop.   Since calls to GETNODE are bound by
$O(n)$ time, the overall time for the procedure is

```
39   PROCEDURE linkup;
40
41      VAR
42         arc : arcpoint;
43
44      BEGIN
45      new(arc);   arc↑.link := node↑.arclink;
46      node↑.arclink := arc;   arc↑.arcname := j
47      END { of linkup }
48
49   BEGIN
50   nodelist := NIL;  reset(nodedata);
51   WHILE NOT eof(nodedata) DO
52      BEGIN
53      readln(i,j);  getpointer(i, node);   linkup
54      END;
55   END { of program }.
```

Figure 8.8.   A procedure to create a linked representation of a graph

$$O(\ a*n^2\ )\ .$$

Although the procedure in figure 8.9 has a higher time cost, the result is a more efficient linked representation of a graph. Specifically, since pointers rather than just the names of nodes appear in the ARCRECORDs, any program processing the graph can access the node record corresponding to a given arc record in a constant amount of time. A procedure processing the arc records created by the procedure in figure 8.8 requires time $O(n)$ to access the node that corresponds to a given arc record. If the speed up procedure would not have been utilized, the program would have to search the list of nodes each time it wished to find the record that corresponded to a node listed in an arc record. There is a favorable trade-off between the processing performed by the speed-up procedure and the rest of the program. By spending some time putting the data into the right order, there is an enormous potential savings in the body of the program, especially for larger and more complex graphs.

8:5. Some Graph Problems

Once an appropriate graph representation is decided upon, many graph problems can be tackled. Many graph problems use labelled graphs. A **labelled graph** is a graph where values are corresponded to arcs and/or nodes. These labels can be handled in the table and RECORD representations of graphs quite easily. For example, suppose a graphical representation of a

```
1    PROGRAM linkedgraph (input, output, nodedata );
2
3    TYPE
4        charstring = PACKED ARRAY [1..8] OF char;
5        nodepoint = ↑noderecord;
6        arcpoint = ↑arcrecord;
7        noderecord = RECORD
8                            nodelink : nodepoint;
9                            name : charstring
10                           arclist : arcpoint
11                    END;
12       arcrecord = RECORD
13                          link : arcpoint;
14                          arcto : nodepoint
15                    END;
16
17   VAR
18       node, nodelist : nodepoint;
19       i, j : charstring;
20       nodedata : text;
21
22   PROCEDURE getpointer ( x : charstring;
23                          VAR point : nodepoint );
24
25       VAR
26           point : nodepoint;
27
28       BEGIN
29       point := nodelist;
30       WHILE ( point <> NIL ) AND ( point↑.name <> x ) DO
31           point := point↑.nodelink;
32       IF point = NIL THEN
33           BEGIN
34           new(point);  point↑.name := x;
35           point↑.nodelink := nodelist;  nodelist := point
36           END
37       END { of getpointer }
38          { CONTINUED ON THE NEXT PAGE }
```

map is desired and we wish to label each country with the color that is used to color that country. The record representation for the nodes might look like

```
39   PROCEDURE linkup;
40
41      VAR
42          arc : arcpoint;
43          other : nodepoint;
44
45      BEGIN
46      new(arc);  arc↑.link := node↑.arclink;  node↑.arclink := arc;
47      getpointer (j, other);  arc↑.arcto := other
48      END { of linkup }
49
50   BEGIN { of program }
51   nodelist := NIL; reset(nodedata);
52   WHILE NOT eof(nodedata) DO
53      BEGIN
54      readln(i,j);  getpointer(i, node);  linkup
55      END
56   END { of program }.
```

Figure 8.9. An alternate procedure to create a linked representation of a graph

```
TYPE
     noderecord = RECORD
                       link : ↑noderecord;
                       arcto : ↑arcrecord;
                       color : charstring
               END;
```

and the arc records would indicate the countries which have a common border with a given country.

Two classical graph problems are the four color problem and the border crossing problem. In the four color problem, a map must be colored with only four colors in such a way that no two countries with a common border are colored with the same color. Two countries that meet at a point are not considered to have a common border. The border crossing problem finds a shortest path, fewest border crossings, in a graph between two given vertices. A shortest path is not necessarily unique. Algorithms can be described for solving both problems without forcing a particular representation for the graph.

Figure 8.10 contains a pseudocode description of an algorithm that solves the border crossing problem. The problem is solved by building a tree structure from the information in the graph. Let A and B be the vertices in a graph for which a shortest path is to be found. The tree is built with A as the root node and all nodes that are linked to A in the graph are made children of A in the tree. This creates the next level of the tree. All the nodes at this level of the tree are connected to A by a path of length one. Now, all

To find a shortest path from node A to node B (level-by-level search):

```
1     Place A at the root of the tree
2     Place A in the queue
3     DO until success or until the queue is empty
4     :   Deque a node, call it X
5     :   FOR each node linked to X by an arc in the graph, DO
6     :   :   IF the node is not already in the tree then
7     :   :       place the node in the tree
8     :   :       enque the node
9     :   :       IF the node is B
10    :   :           indicate success
11    :   :       ENDIF
12    :   :   ENDIF
13    :   ENDFOR
14    ENDDO
```

Figure 8.10.   A Border Crossing Algorithm

the nodes at this level are processed the same way A was processed to produce all the nodes on the next level of the tree. This next level contains all the nodes that have a path of length 2 to A. By building the tree in this way, when the node B is first encountered, a shortest path from A to B is found.

Figure 8.11 illustrates the relationship between a graph and the tree built by the algorithm in figure 8.10. The algorithm builds the tree a level at a time, constructing all paths of length one from A, then all paths of length 2, and so forth. In order to reduce the size of the tree, multiple occurrences of nodes are not placed in the tree. This reduces the time and space requirements of the algorithm. The ability of the algorithm to find a shortest path is not modified because each node is placed in the tree only the first time it is encountered. Therefore, the tree contains at least one of the shortest paths between each node in the tree and the root of the tree.

Figure 8.12 contains a pseudocode description of an algorithm that 4-colors a graph. The algorithm uses two stacks; one stack contains the nodes that need to be colored, NOCOLOR, and the other stack contains those nodes that have been successfully colored, OK. Initially, no node is colored, OK is empty. Then the algorithm attempts to color the nodes with four colors.

Stacks are not an important component of this problem. What is important is that some structure keeps the nodes in the two distinct groupings, NOCOLOR and OK. An exercise problem suggests a method for keeping the nodes organized with a doubly linked list.

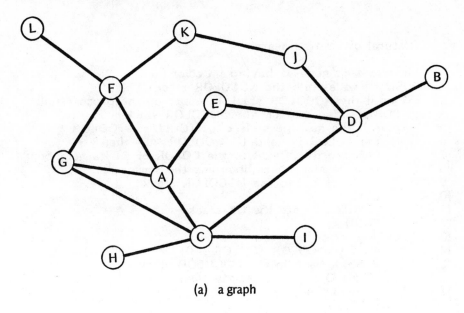

(a) a graph

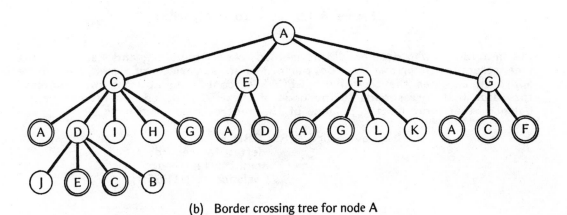

(b) Border crossing tree for node A

Figure 8.11. A graph and its border crossing tree

8:6. AVL Tree Restructuring

Binary trees are very useful structures. This section describes a tree restructuring process called the AVL tree balancing algorithm. It is named after

(Natural order tree search)

```
 1   Indicate each node as having no color
 2   PUSH all nodes into the NOCOLOR stack
 3   DO until the NOCOLOR stack is empty or the process fails
 4   :   POP a node, X, from the NOCOLOR stack
 5   :   give X the next possible color (COLOR := COLOR + 1)
 6   :   IF the COLOR is valid (0 < COLOR < 5) then
 7   :       Compare its COLOR to the COLOR of all its neighbors
 8   :       IF at least one neighbor has the same color
 9   :           PUSH X into the NOCOLOR stack
10   :       ELSE
11   :           PUSH X into the OK stack
12   :       ENDIF
13   :   ELSE
14   :       clear the COLOR (COLOR = 0)
15   :       PUSH X back to the NOCOLOR stack
16   :       IF the OK stack is empty then
17   :           report failure
18   :       ELSE
19   :           POP a node from the OK stack and
20   :           PUSH it onto the NOCOLOR stack
21   :       ENDIF
22   :   ENDIF
23   ENDDO
```

Figure 8.12. A 4-Color Algorithm

the individuals who developed this method, Adelson-Velskii and Landis. This tree structure algorithm can be performed in a variety of ways. A simple approach allocates the tree using RECORDs containing at least two pointers, the value that corresponds to the node of the RECORD, and an integer value, balance, that indicates the balance of the subtree below the node.

```
avlrecord = RECORD
                left : ↑avlrecord;
                right : ↑avlrecord;
                balance : INTEGER;
                    . . .
            END;    .
```

Figure 8.13 illustrates a binary tree of values that satisfies several important properties:

1. All the values in the left subtree of any node are less than or equal to the value in the node;
2. All the values in the right subtree of any node are greater than or equal to the value of the node;

3. The absolute value of the difference in length between the longest
    path from a node through its left subtree and the longest path
    through its right subtree is at most one.

The first two properties create a nice relationship between the nodes in a
tree and make it easy to write an algorithm which searches through the tree
to determine if a given value appears as a node in the tree.   Writing this algorithm is left as an exercise.

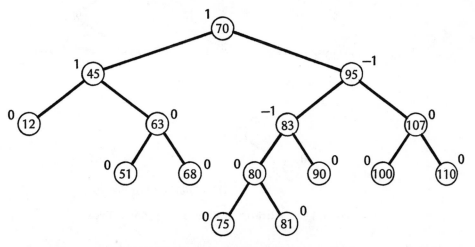

Figure 8.13.   A balanced binary tree

A program that searches through this tree for a given value performs in time
bound by the length of the longest path in the tree.   For a tree of n nodes,
the ideal time would be O(log n).   This would occur if the tree had

$$2^k$$

nodes at level k.   This is the purpose of the third property, namely, to keep
the length of the longest path as short as possible.

The **balance** of a node is the length of the longest path down its right subtree minus the length of the longest path down its left subtree.   Figure 8.13
illustrates a binary tree that satisfies the relations described above.   The
number written above each node is its balance.   Suppose new values are
added to the tree.   For example, if the number 30 is added to the tree, the
result would be as it appears in figure 8.14a.   If the value 72 is then added,
then the result is figure 8.14b.

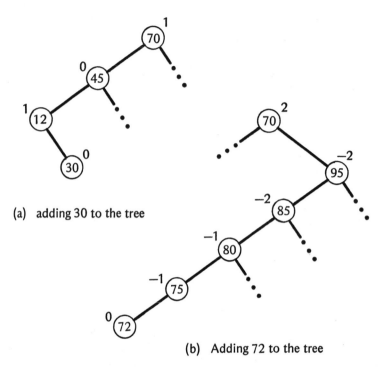

(a) adding 30 to the tree

(b) Adding 72 to the tree

Figure 8.14. Adding nodes to an AVL Tree

The AVL tree rebalancing process keeps the balances of all the nodes as -1, 0, and 1. Under this restriction, the result in figure 8.14b is not tolerable. The tree should be restructured so that all nodes have balances of -1, 0, or 1. It is desirable for the rebalancing routine to be efficient. That is, it should not use much time or space. The time should be at most

O(length of the longest path in the tree).

As new nodes are added to the tree, the nodes in the path between the new node and the root must be rebalanced. This is done as follows. Set the balance of the new node to zero, then repeat the following steps, starting at the node above the new node:

    a.   Add 1 to the balance if the path from the new node comes up the right subtree of the node being balanced;

    b.   Subtract 1 from the balance of the node if the path from the new node comes up the left subtree of the node being balanced;

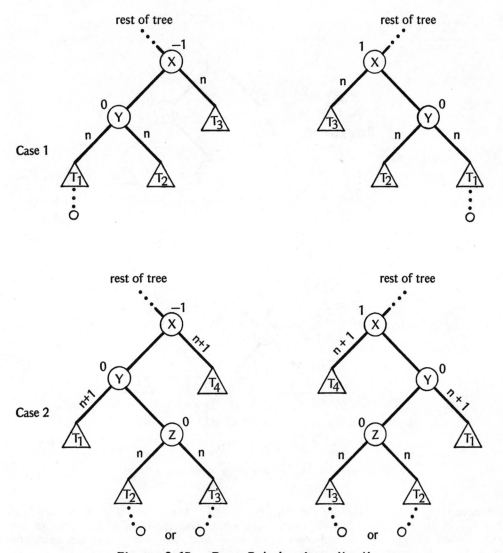

Figure 8.15.   Four Rebalancing situations

c.   Proceed up the path towards the root to the next node if the absolute value of the balance of this node has been increased, otherwise stop rebalancing nodes.

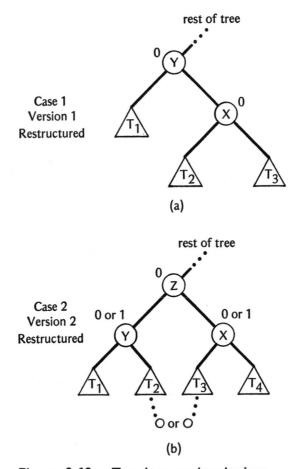

Figure 8.16.   Two tree restructurings

Unfortunately, as indicated in figure 8.14b, the balancing can get out of hand. It is important to observe that once the balance of a node is set to zero, none of the nodes between that node and the root must be rebalanced. It is this observation that makes the AVL tree rebalancing nice.

The AVL tree restructuring recognizes two restructuring cases. Each of these cases has two symmetric versions, see figure 8.15. The triangles,

$$T_1, \ T_2, \ T_3, \ \text{and} \ T_4$$

represent the subtrees of the indicated nodes. The balances indicate the balances of the nodes before the new node is placed in the tree. The value n or n+1 on the arc to each subtree indicates the length of the longest path from the node through the subtree before the new node was added.

The relationship between the restructurings of the versions of the cases is symmetrical. Here, the restructurings of the first versions are described and the second versions are left as an exercise. In the second case, the restructuring is the same regardless of which subtree contains the new node. The difference is only in the rebalancing of the nodes after the restructuring. Figure 8.16 illustrates the rebalancings of the first versions of both cases. The assumption is that node X is the first node that is about to be rebalanced with a value of -2 or 2. Since only balancings of -1, 0, or 1 are allowed, the subtree beginning with node X in figure 8.15a is restructured as indicated in figure 8.16a. The nodes X and Y then have the indicated balances. Since Y is now the root of this subtree and its balance is zero, there is no need to proceed up the tree and rebalance any more nodes.

The restructuring is a straightforward process. If XPOINT and YPOINT are pointers to the records containing X and Y and LEFT and RIGHT are the pointer components in the X and Y records to their respective left and right subtrees, then a code sequence like

```
XPOINT↑.LEFT := YPOINT↑.RIGHT;
POINTTOX := YPOINT;
XPOINT↑.BALANCE := 0;
YPOINT↑.BALANCE := 0
```

where POINTTOX is the pointer that would have been pointing to the subtree whose root was X.

In case 2, the tree is restructured as indicated by figure 8.16b. Here, a code sequence like

```
XPOINT↑.LEFT := ZPOINT↑.RIGHT;
YPOINT↑.RIGHT := ZPOINT↑.LEFT;
POINTTOX := ZPOINT;
ZPOINT↑.LEFT := YPOINT;
ZPOINT↑.RIGHT := XPOINT;
ZPOINT↑.BALANCE := 0;
IF the new node was added to the left subtree of Z
    YPOINT↑.BALANCE := 0;
    XPOINT↑.BALANCE := 1;
ELSE IF the new node was added to the right subtree of Z
    YPOINT↑.BALANCE := 1;
    XPOINT↑.BALANCE := 0;
ELSE
    YPOINT↑.BALANCE := 0;
    XPOINT↑.BALANCE := 0;
```

The rebalancing process uses a pushdown stack. As new nodes are placed on the tree, pointers to the nodes along the path from the root to the new node are pushed into a stack to save the information about the location of the path in the tree. This stack is where the pointers XPOINT, YPOINT, ZPOINT, and POINTTOX came from in the discussion above. Also, for each node in the path, information must be kept regarding which subtree below the node contains the new node. This information can also be pushed into a stack, or, by using the relations that exist between nodes to determine which subtree of a particular node is being processed. The details of carrying this out are left as an exercise.

Another binary tree search and update scheme that shares the basic tree organization of the AVL tree is the B-tree file organization method. B+-trees and B*-trees are variations of B-tree organization that organize information into binary trees and efficiently maintain the tree structure. Various keyed file structures, that is, access to data stored on disks using a line number or some other key to access a single record, are often organized with a B-tree like structure to quickly access individual records. A typical example is IBM VSAM files. The scope of this topic goes beyond the purpose and level of this text. There is much in the current literature about this topic.

8:7. EXERCISES

1. Write procedures to accept graphic information in an appropriate form, store it in a matrix, print the matrix, and determine basic connection information between nodes. For example, write a logical procedure CONNECT(I,J) which is true if a path exists between I and J, otherwise it is false.

2. Find a time bound relative to the number of nodes n in a digraph for the procedures designed in problem 1.

3. Write procedures as in problem 1 for representing a graph in a triangular matrix.

4. Time the triangular matrix routines written in exercise 3.

5. What is the exact number of non-zero locations in a matrix representation of a graph of the contiguous United States?

6. What is the space utilization of the table representation of a map of the contiguous United States?

7. What is the number of multiplications and additions performed in a matrix multiplication of an n by n matrix?

8. Write procedures to represent digraphs using the table approach. Assume that character strings are used as the names of node in the digraph. Write a speed-up procedure like the speed-up procedure for the list representation of digraphs which keeps in the table an index to the row of the table that corresponds to the other vertex of the arc. To do this, it is convenient to keep an array of character strings to keep the names of the nodes and that the index to the location of the name is also the index to the row of the table which contains the arc information.

9. Assume that the input of pairs to the table building procedure represents a graph rather than a digraph. That is, each pair is an unordered rather than an ordered pair and hence two entries must be made in the table. Write a modification of the input procedure to handle this by storing the graph arc information as if each arc in the graph is represented by two arcs in a digraph, one pointed in each direction.

10. Do exercise problem 9 for the linked representation.

11. Write and measure a program that four colors a map of the United States using records. Modify the linked allocation procedure for a graph so that the nodes are placed in a doubly linkled list structure. Also, place in each node record a component for the node's color. Carry out the equivalent of the algorithm in figure 8.12 using a pointer that traverses the doubly linked list. Each time a node is successfully colored, the pointer follows the forward link to the next record, and every time a node is not successfully colored, the pointer resets the node's color to zero and follows the reverse link back to recolor the previous node.

12. Perform exercise 11 using a table representation of the graph.

13. Perform the Border Crossing Problem using records.

14. Perform the Border Crossing Problem using tables and a vector representation of the graph. Write a program to carry out the border crossing problem as follows: Build two arrays as indicated in figure 8.17 to simultaneously represent the nodes in the tree, the linkage of the nodes in the tree, and the contents of the queue. Figure 8.17 indicates the status of the tree and the queue when that part of the tree in figure 8.11 up to the processing of node C has occurred. The values in the array BRANCH indicate the tree linkage, that is, the nodes in locations 2 through 5 all have their corresponding BRANCH values as one to indicate that they are all linked to the node in location one, A. The pointers F and R indicate, respectively, the current front and the current rear of the queue.

15. Figure 8.18 can be thought of as representing a flow network with BEGIN as the source and END as the sink. The number on each arc represents the maximum flow through that arc. Given the flow limitations on each arc, what is the maximum flow that can go from the source to the sink? Describe a computer representation for this graphical information.

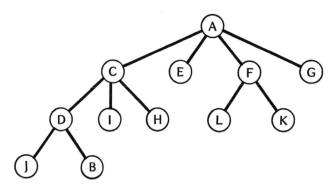

(a)   Reduced tree of Figure 8.11

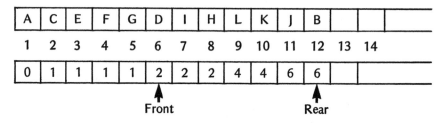

(b)   Tree and queue

Figure 8.17.   A vector representation of a tree and queue

Write a brief description of the difficulty that is encountered in this problem. Write a program to evaluate and solve problems of this type.

16. Another interpretation that can be given to the numerical values in figure 8.18 is the number of days it takes to traverse the arc. Write a program that finds the path from BEGIN to END whose sum of the arc values is maximum.

17. With the same view as in problem 16, write a program that finds the path whose sum of the arc values is minimum.

18. Design an AVL algorithm to perform a tree rebalancing and, when necessary, restructure the tree. Carefully consider the problem of properly handling a restructuring which would change the root of the tree. This is a typical failure of AVL algorithms. Write a program that performs a natural order tree search through the AVL tree and print the nodes in the tree in the order in which they are first encountered. If the AVL tree is in proper order, all nodes should be printed in their proper collating order. Be sure that your algorithm empties its pushdown stack every time it is finished inserting a new node in the tree. Test your al-

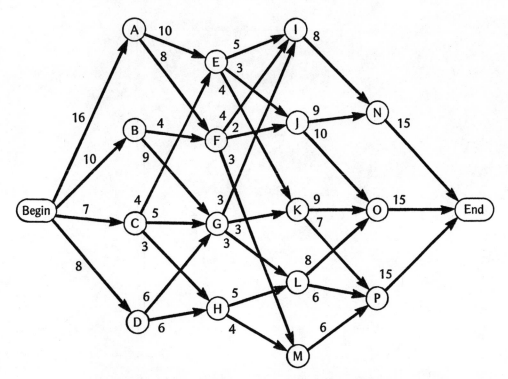

Figure 8.18. A Labeled Digraph

gorithms with the following sequence of input, 50, 100, 200, 300, 95, 90, 85, 30, 35, 40, 45, 25, 20, 15, 70, 75, 86, 69, 66, 63, 150, 205, 175, 190.

19. Do a literature search on B-trees and B*-trees algorithms. Find and implement an algorithm for one of them.

9

Sorting

The amount of computer time spent sorting information is enormous. There are many sorting techniques with a variety of timing characteristics. Some methods have very interesting timing characteristics, where in general the timing might be poor, $O(N^2)$, but in some special circumstances, the timing can be excellent, $O(N)$. For example, in general, the bubble sort that is described later in this chapter has poor timing characteristics. But when the numbers are almost in sorted order, the results are excellent. It is this observation that leads to the Shell sort.

There are two categories of sorting problems that we shall refer to as sorting and updating. By **sorting** we mean methods where all of the information is unorganized and must be placed in some order. The **update** category contains algorithms which handle collections of information that are already in order and must be revised as the new information is inserted. Update methods are discussed in the next chapter along with searching. Sorting methods are described in this chapter.

9:1. Selection and Exchange Methods

Two categories of sorting techniques that are easy to describe and carry out are the selection and exchange methods. These methods approach sorting from two different points of view. In a selection method, a position in an array is selected, then the item that belongs in that position is found. A selection sort procedure is illustrated in figure 9.1. In this sort procedure, the outer loop selects a position i, then the inner loop finds the position, k, of the value that should go into the i-th position. The timing of this procedure is given by the formula

```
1   PROGRAM selectsort (input, output );
2
3   TYPE
4       anarray = ARRAY [ 1..1000 ] OF integer;
5
6   PROCEDURE select ( VAR value : anarray; size : integer );
7
8       VAR
9           i, j, k, extra : integer;
10
11      BEGIN
12      FOR i := 1 TO size - 1 DO
13          BEGIN
14          k := i;
15          FOR j := i+1 TO size DO
16              IF value [j] < value [k] THEN
17                  k := j;
18          IF i <> k THEN
19              BEGIN
20              extra := value [i];   value [i] := value [k];
21              value [k] := extra
22              END
23          END
24      END;
```

Figure 9.1.   A Selection Sort

$$\int_{1}^{SIZE-1} \int_{I+1}^{SIZE} dj\ di$$

$$= \int_{1}^{SIZE-1} (SIZE - I - 1)\ dI$$

$$= (SIZE - 1) i - i^2/2$$

$$= O((SIZE - 1)^2/2).$$

This means that this sort has $O(n^2/2)$ timing.

An important observation about this procedure is the rigidity of its timing. That is, the loops execute a specific predetermined number of times regardless of the order of the data. This is not the case for the sort illustrated in figure 9.2.

```
1    PROGRAM bubblesort (input, output );
2
3    TYPE
4        anarray = ARRAY [1..1000] OF integer;
5
6    PROCEDURE bubble ( VAR value : anarray; size : integer );
7
8        VAR
9            i, j, extra : integer;
10
11       BEGIN
12       FOR i := 1 TO size-1 DO
13          BEGIN
14          j := i;
15          WHILE (j > 0) AND (value [j] > value [j+1]   )DO
16             BEGIN
17             extra := value [j]; value [j] := value [j+1];
18             value [j+1] := extra;   j := j - 1
19             END
20          END
21       END;
```

Figure 9.2.   A Shuttle Interchange Sort-Bubble Sort

The program illustrated in figure 9.2 is a shuttle exchange sort commonly referred to as a bubble sort. In this procedure each item is moved, or "bubbled-up", to the position in the ordering where it belongs.

The procedure functions as follows: Each time through the outer loop, the index, i, indicates the count of the number of values that have been sorted. The number that is to be bubbled into the order collection appears in position i+1. The inner loop performs the bubbling process with j+1 being the current position of the value being processed.

Timing this procedure is more difficult because the inner loop does not have a simple counter that determines the number of iterations of that loop. As a matter of fact, the number of iterations of the inner loop depends upon the order of the data. For this reason, three timing results are given.

The worst case timing for figure 9.2 occurs when the number being processed must always be bubbled up to the top of the array. This is the case when the input is in reverse order. In this case, the i-th time through the outer loop, the inner loop iterates i times. This produces the timing result

$$\int_{2}^{SIZE} i \; di = O \; (\; SIZE^2/2 \;)$$

Immediately we see that the bubble sort might have some advantage over the selection method. This becomes more apparent by looking at the best case time for the inner loop of the bubble sort. This case occurs when the inner loop never executes. This happens when the data is already in order. In this case, the outer loop executes SIZE-1 times and the bubble sort would execute in O(SIZE) time.

There is a considerable range between these two extreme timings. For this reason, it is worthwhile to consider a third timing to see whether one of these extremes or some time within this range is a more realistic expectation. A reasonable compromise might be the following: Each time through the inner loop, the value being processed, in position i+1, on the average, will be bubbled half way up the set of i ordered values. That is, the inner loop iterates O(i/2) times. This produces the timing

$$\int_{1}^{SIZE - 1} i/2 \; di = O \; (\; SIZE^2/4 \;)$$

This indicates that on the average the bubble sort is twice as fast as the selection sort but they are both

$$O \; (\; n^2 \;)$$

sorting techniques. However, in the case where the data is in order, the bubble sort operates in O(n) time.

9:2. The Shell Sort

Since the bubble sort executes in time O(N) when the numbers are in order, it might be worth considering ways of improving its timing. The problem with the bubble up process is that it bubbles up a value one location at a time. If something could be done to change the step size of the bubbling process so that values are moved in larger steps, the timing might be improved. The program in figure 9.3 does this.

```
1    PROGRAM shellsort ( input, output );
2
3    TYPE
4        anarray = ARRAY [1..1000] OF integer;
5
6    PROCEDURE shell ( VAR a : anarray; size : integer);
7
8        VAR
9            dist, i, j, extra : integer;
10
11       BEGIN
12       dist := size DIV 2;
13       WHILE dist > 0 DO
14           BEGIN
15           FOR i := 1 TO size-dist DO
16               BEGIN
17               j := i;
18               WHILE (j > 0) AND ( a [j] > a [j+dist] ) DO
19                   BEGIN
20                   extra := a [j];   a [j] := a [j+dist];
21                   a [j+dist] := extra;   j := j-dist
22                   END
23               END;
24           dist := dist DIV 2
25           END
26       END;
```

Figure 9.3. A Shell Sort

This procedure (figure 9.3), called the Shell sort, is named after its inventor. The basic concept behind this sort is to put the values almost in order before doing a bubble sort. This is done by considering the array of numbers as several lists of numbers, then bubble sorting those lists. Observe that the inner two loops of figure 9.3 have the same structure as the bubble sort of figure 9.1 with the variable DIST replacing the 1, J+DIST instead of J+1. It is the way the DIST is used that is the key to understanding the Shell sort.

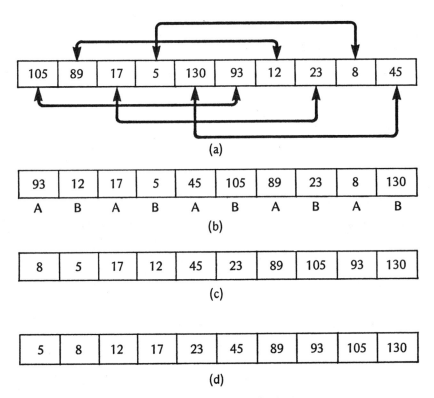

Figure 9.4. Example of Shell Sort

The outer loop of the Shell sort sets the value DIST. Each time through the outer loop, the inner two loops are doing the equivalent of bubble sorting DIST collections of values, each collection containing about SIZE/DIST values. At the beginning DIST is large, therefore the number of values in each collection is relatively small. The "bubblings" of the values in these small lists are actually large movements in the positions of the values in the array.

In order to see how a Shell sort works, consider the array in figure 9.4a. Since the array has 10 positions, initially DIST is 5. Therefore, numbers that are 5 positions apart are compared. If they are not in order, they are switched. The result appears in figure 9.4b and took 5 loop iterations. DIST is then halved,

$$DIST := DIST \ DIV \ 2.$$

The inner two loops of the Shell sort now do the equivalent of bubble sorts on two sets of numbers. The numbers marked A are bubble sorted and the numbers marked B are separately bubble sorted. This takes 17 loop iterations and the result appears in figure 9.4c. Once again DIST is halved and becomes 1. Now the inner two loops perform a bubble sort on the whole collection of values. But the numbers are all close to where they belong. Therefore, this bubble sort takes only 13 loop iterations. Counting the three iterations of the outer loop, the array is sorted in only 38 loop iterations, which is very close to

$$10 * \log 10.$$

The concept behind this sort is that as DIST becomes smaller, the numbers will get close to their correct order, hence each time through the bubble sort of the inner two loops, its timing will be close to O(SIZE). Each time through the outer loop, DIST is divided by 2, therefore, the outer loop iterates

$$O (LOG_2 \ SIZE)$$

times and the best one could expect from the Shell sort is

$$O(N \log N)$$

time.

SIZE OF THE ARRAY	BUBBLE TIME	SHELL TIME
100 RANDOM VALUES	2427	1128
200 RANDOM VALUES	10946	2743
400 RANDOM VALUES	41087	5894
200 VALUES IN ORDER	200	1528
200 VALUES IN REVERSE ORDER	20000	3064

Figure 9.5.   Timing comparisons - Bubble vs. Shell

Interestingly, although the Shell sort has been around for some time, no one has been able to gain a good theoretical handle on its timing. But in fact, the Shell sort does produce good timing results. The table in figure 9.5 illustrates some timings for the Shell sort and Bubble sort on various sized collections of random numbers and the two extreme cases (order and reverse order). From this, one can see that the timing characteristics of the Shell sort make it more desirable than either of the two sorts described in section 9:1.

```
1    PROGRAM treesorting ( input, output );
2
3    TYPE
4       anarray = ARRAY[1..1000] OF integer;
5
6    PROCEDURE treesort ( VAR a : anarray;
7                            size : integer );
8
9       PROCEDURE tree1;
10
11         VAR
12            parent, child , extra, i : integer;
13
14         BEGIN { of tree 1 }
15         FOR i := 2 TO size DO
16            BEGIN
17            child := i;  parent := i div 2;
18            WHILE ( parent > 0 ) AND ( a [child] > a [parent] ) DO
19               BEGIN
20               extra := a [child];  a [child] := a [parent];
21               a [parent] := extra; child := parent;
22               parent := parent div 2
23               END
24            END
25         END { of tree 1 };
26         { CONTINUED ON NEXT PAGE }
```

9:3. Quicksort and Treesort

The quicksort was described in 4:2 and the treesort (or heapsort) in 4:3.
These two sorts have excellent timing characteristics. The tree sort, see
figure 9.6, was written as two procedures, one to organize the tree and the
second to perform the sort. Each part executes in time

$$O (N \log N)$$

and so the whole procedure executes in time

$$O (2*N \log N).$$

The quicksort (figure 9.7) has an average timing of $O (N * \log N)$. However both sorts have an undesirable characteristic in that neither sort takes
advantage of the existing order of the data. As a matter of fact, the worst
case timing for the quicksort occurs when the numbers are already in order.
In that case, the timing is

$$O (N^2).$$

```
27        PROCEDURE tree 2;
28
29           VAR
30              i, locate, key : integer;
31              place : boolean;
32
33           BEGIN { of tree 2 }
34           FOR i := size DOWNTO 2 DO
35              BEGIN
36              key := a [i];  a [i] := a [1];
37              locate := 1;   place := false;
38              WHILE NOT place DO
39                 BEGIN
40                 firstchild := 2*locate;
41                 IF ( firstchild >= i )
42                    OR ( ( firstchild+1 >= i )
43                       AND ( key >= a [firstchild] ) )
44                    OR ( ( key >= a [firstchild] )
45                       AND ( key >= a [firstchild+1] ) ) THEN
46                    BEGIN
47                    place := true; a [locate] := key
48                    END
49                 ELSE
50                    IF ( (firstchild+1 >= i) AND (a [firstchild] >= key) )
51                       OR ( ( a [firstchild] >= key )
52                         AND (a [firstchild] >= a [firstchild+1] ) )THEN
53                       BEGIN
54                       a [locate] := a [firstchild];
55                       locate := firstchild
56                       END
57                    ELSE
58                       BEGIN
59                       a [locate] := a [firstchild+1];
60                       locate := firstchild+1
61                       END
62                 END
63              END
64           END { of tree 2 };
65
66        BEGIN { of tree sort }
67        tree1;   tree2
68        END { of tree sort };
```

Figure 9.6.   A Heapsort Algorithm

To see this, observe that the value used as the KEY in the sort process is placed back in the position it was in.   This is a disadvantage in the quick-sort, because the quicksort, in placing the KEY back into the array, has its best timing result if the array is split into two equal parts.

```
1   PROGRAM quicksort (input, output);
2
3   TYPE
4      anarray = ARRAY [ 1..5000 ] OF integer;
5      stackrecord = RECORD
6                            link: ↑stackrecord;
7                             min: integer;
8                             max: integer
9                    END;
10
11  PROCEDURE quick ( VAR a: anarray;
12                         n: integer);
13
14     TYPE
15        dset = (up, down);
16
17     VAR
18        direction: dset;
19        key, high, low, lowup, highdown: integer;
20        top, stack: ↑stackrecord;
21
22     PROCEDURE push ( first, second: integer);
23
24        BEGIN
25        new (top);  top↑.link := stack;  stack := top;
26        stack↑.max := second;  stack↑.min := first
27        END;
28             {  CONTINUED ON THE NEXT PAGE  }
```

This fault in the quicksort can be improved upon by creating a selection process for determinng the KEY. One typical selection process is to look at three values within the range that is sorted, then use the middle of the three values as the key. For example, it would be relatively easy to write a procedure that compares the first, last, and center value in the range, then uses the middle collating value as the KEY.

This modification is suggested as an exercise. To see its timing characteristics, the table in figure 9.8 illustrates some loop timing comparisons between the quicksort and the variation that is suggested here.

```
29      BEGIN { of quick }
30        stack := NIL;  push (1, n );
31        WHILE stack <> NIL DO
32          BEGIN
33          low := stack↑.min;  high := stack↑.max;  top := stack;
34          stack := stack↑.lin;  release (top);
35          IF low < high THEN
36            BEGIN
37            lowup := low;  highdown := high;
38            direction := down;  key := a [low];
39            WHILE lowup <> highdown DO
40              BEGIN
41              IF direction = down THEN
42                IF key < a [highdown] THEN
43                  highdown := highdown - 1
44                ELSE BEGIN
45                  a [lowup] := a [highdown];
46                  direction := up
47                END
48              ELSE
49                IF key > a [lowup] THEN
50                  lowup := lowup + 1
51                ELSE BEGIN
52                  a [highdown] := a [lowup]
53                  direction := down
54                END
55              END;
56            IF (high - highdown) > (lowup - low) THEN
57              BEGIN   push ( highdown + 1, high );
58              push ( low, lowup - 1 )   END
59            ELSE  BEGIN
60              push ( low, lowup - 1 );  push ( highdown + 1, high )
61              END
62            END
63          END
64      END { of quick };
```

Figure 9.7.   A Quicksort procedure

9:4. Merging

It can be mathematically shown that the best timing one can expect in a worst case for a sort procedure is

$$O (N \log N).$$

SIZE OF THE ARRAY	QUICK TIME	QUICKER TIME
100 RANDOM VALUES	937	713
200 RANDOM VALUES	1609	1582
400 RANDOM VALUES	3751	3524
200 VALUES IN ORDER	20000	1553
200 VALUES IN REVERSE ORDER	20000	1553

Figure 9.8.   Timing comparisons-quicksort vs. quickersort

The generalization of the merge sort described as an exercise in chapter 6 produces this timing. In concept, this sort is fairly easy to describe, but in fact, it is a little difficult to carry out.

Figure 9.9 illustrates how a merge sort works. In an ideal generalized merge sort, the N values that are sorted initially form N lists of one value, as in the first level of figure 9.9. These N lists are sorted pairwise into N/2 lists of 2 values, and the result is illustrated by the second level of figure 9.9b. These N/2 lists are sorted pairwise into N/4 lists of 4 values, which takes us down to the next level in the figure. This process is continued until the result is 1 list of N values as in the one list at the bottom of figure 9.9. At each step in the merging process, there are at most O(N) comparisons. Since the process starts with N lists of 1 value and the number of lists is halved each time, the process will be repeated O(log N) times. Hence the whole process executes in time

$$O (N \log N).$$

Figure 9.10 illustrates a basic merging procedure. This procedure merges two one-way grounded lists. The procedure has three distinct components. First, the procedure initializes itself by releasing the smallest value from one list and setting the NEWTOP pointer to it. Second, the loop performs the basic merging process. Finally, after one list becomes NIL, the rest of the items in the other list are linked to the bottom of the new list.

This merge procedure is a parallel, using lists, of a three tape merging process. That is, given three magnetic tape drives, one can merge two sorted collections of data, stored on two magnetic tapes, onto a tape mounted on a third drive. A look at tape oriented sorts can give us some appreciation of the practical considerations one must face when programming, specifically, in this case, the physical sequential limitations of magnetic tapes.

An important tape oriented sort procedure is the polyphase merge sort. There are many variations of this technique. Usually the sort feature that is incorporated into COBOL compilers or supplied as part of the operating system's sort processor on many computers is a type of polyphase merge. In

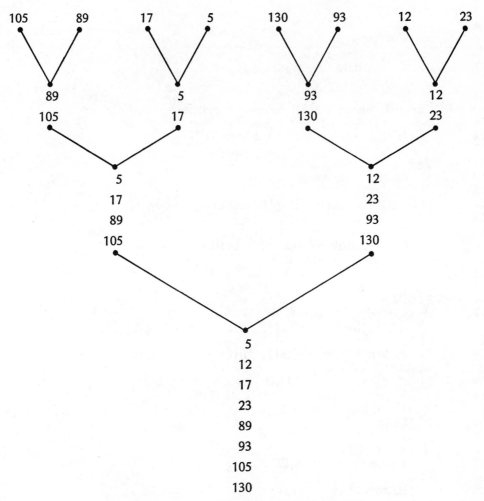

Figure 9.9. A Merge Sort Illustration

order to understand the basic structure of a polyphase merge, consider the situation in which three tape drives and a limited amount of memory are available. The polyphase merge consists of two main phases. During the first phase the procedure sorts, within its limited memory, small subsets of the numbers that are to be sorted. These sorted subsets are written onto tapes as files of data. The first phase repeats this process writing files onto two of the three available tapes until all the values have been placed into files on two of the tapes, see figure 9.11a.

```
1    PROGRAM mergesort ( input, output );
2
3    TYPE
4       pointer = ↑list;
5       list = RECORD
6                   link : pointer;
7                   data : integer
8               END;
9
10   PROCEDURE merge ( VAR newlist : pointer;
11                     VAR list1 : pointer;
12                     VAR list2 : pointer );
13
14       VAR
15           bottom : pointer;
16
17       PROCEDURE release ( VAR oldlist : pointer );
18
19           BEGIN
20           bottom↑.link := oldlist;    bottom := oldlist;
21           oldlist := oldlist↑.link
22           END;
23
24       BEGIN
25       IF list1↑.data <= list2↑.data THEN
26           BEGIN bottom := list1;   list1 := list1↑.link  END
27       ELSE
26           BEGIN bottom := list2;   list2 := list2↑.link  END;
29       newlist := bottom;
30       WHILE (list1 <> NIL) AND (list2 <> NIL) DO
31           IF list1 ↑.data <= list2↑.data THEN
32               release ( list1 )
33           ELSE
34               release ( list2 );
35       IF list1 = NIL THEN
36           bottom↑.link := list2
37       ELSE
38           bottom↑.link := list1
39       END;
```

Figure 9.10. Merging Two Lists of Records

The second phase merges pairs of files from two tapes forming larger sorted files onto the third tape. This process is repeated until one of the tapes is emptied, see figure 9.11b. At this point the merging process switches resources and uses the emptied tape as its new output device and the tape that had been the output tape is now used for input (figure 9.11c). This process is continued, switching between tapes, until one file is formed on a single tape and the entire set of data is sorted (figures 9.11c and 9.11d).

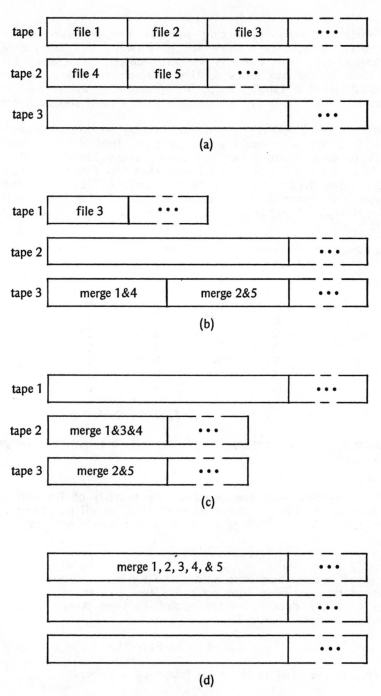

Figure 9.11. Setting up a polyphase merge

Any appropriate in-memory sorting process can be used during the first phase. The entire process is very straightforward and lends itself to a fairly direct coding effort. But there is one little catch: How many files should be placed on each of the two tapes so that the second phase can easily produce one sorted file on one tape? Once this question is answered, another question is also answered, namely, which tape will contain the final result?

The answers to these questions are obtained by working backwards, see figure 9.12. To finish with one file on one tape, that file is obtained by merging one file on each of the other two tapes, see 9.12a to 9.12d. Now assume the one file on tape 2 (figure 9.12b) was obtained from merging one file from each of the other tapes. This leads to figure 9.12c. Continuing, the two files on tape 3 of figure 9.12c were formed from 2 files each on the other two tapes. Repeating this process yields the results listed on subsequent lines in figure 9.12.

	TAPE 1	TAPE 2	TAPE 3
A	1	0	0
B	0	1	1
C	1	0	2
D	3	2	0
E	0	5	3
F	5	0	8
G	13	8	0

Number of Files on Each Tape

Figure 9.12. Working backwards to start a polyphase merge sort

The number that describes the count of the number of files on the tape with the most files is the sum of the number of files on all the tapes in the previous line in figure 9.12. This is repeated continuously yielding the numbers

$$1, \ 1, \ 2, \ 3, \ 5, \ 8, \ 13, \ \ldots \ ,$$

which is a well known sequence called the Fibonacci sequence. As a result, if one wishes to distribute files on tapes two and three so that the process terminates with the data in sorted order on tape one, then the number of files on tapes 2 and 3 should be

$$F(3i-1) \text{ and } F(3i-2),$$

respectively, where $F(n)$ is the n-th Fibonacci number.

9:5. Two Special Case Sorting Methods

There is a considerable amount of literature on sorting methods, their timings, and various special considerations. Here, two cases are illustrated which take advantage of the storage medium or the data space available. The first method might be a bit dated, but it demonstrates how one storage medium, cards, was used advantageously.

The first method is commonly referred to as a radix sort. It sorts values on 80 column cards using a card sorter. An 80 column card contains 12 rows with information stored by punching holes in various columns. A card sorter contains 13 trays into which cards are fed from a single input hopper. The card sorter works by being set to sort the cards according to the values in one card column. The cards are then directed into one of the 13 trays, one each per card row, and one tray for errors.

Assume that a deck of cards is to be sorted using a number that appears in n specific columns. The card sorter would be set to sort according to the least significant column and the cards run through the sorter. The cards are removed from the trays, starting with tray 0 through tray 9, placed back into the input hopper and resorted using the next more significant column. After all columns are processed, the cards are in order.

In n columns, a card can contain

$$K = 10^N$$

values. If K cards are processed, the time would be

$$O (K \, LOG_{10} \, K)$$

using a radix sort on a card sorter.

Another special method is the address calculation sort. This sort attempts to calculate the index to the location where a value is to be placed. This calculation is performed knowing the size of the array and the distribution of the numbers being sorted. But this method is also a searching method and is described in detail in the next chapter.

9:6. EXERCISES

1. Write the modification of the quicksort described in section 9.3.

2. In the Shell sort, experiment with various methods of determining DIST so that two consecutive values are always relatively prime, except that the last value used for DIST is one. Do this by setting aside a small array of distances, for example, the sequence, 1, 2, 5, 7, 17, 31, 63, etc.

3. Experiment with the bubble sort by sorting arrays that are "almost" in order.

4. Suppose interchanging values in an array could be costly. Compare the bubble, selection, and Shell sorts under this criterion.

5. Write and test a polyphase merge sort.

6. Determine the number of files that would have to be written onto tapes if 4 tape drives were available for a polyphase merge sort.

7. Determine the number of files that can be conveniently used to perform a polyphase merge with n tape drives.

10

Search and Update

Given a collection of information and a single item of data, how much time is required to determine if the item is in the collection? Or, if the collection is kept in some order, how much time is required to update the collection by inserting the item? Search and update problems consume enormous amounts of computer time. By search problems we mean the problems of determinimg if an item is in some collection of data. By updating we mean the problem of reorganizing a collection of information to include a single new item or several new items. In this chapter, several basic search and update techniques are described. These techniques form the base for many searching and updating methods. The assumption in this chapter is that the collection of information can be conveniently handled in memory. In reality, most large collections of information are kept on pseudorandom access devices (disks, drums, etc.) which have timing considerations that are different from memory access timing. But, these techniques form a solid foundation from which other methods can be viewed and judged.

10:1. Sequential Search and Update

Assume that a collection of information is stored in an array and a value in ITEM. To determine if ITEM is in the array, the simplest search method to program sequentially steps through the array comparing ITEM to the values in the array. Figure 10.1 illustrates this assuming that the array is not organized. Figure 10.2 illustrates the same sort assuming the values in the array are in increasing collating order.

There are several questions that should be answered regarding the timing of search procedures:

1. What is the best possible time?
2. What is the worst possible time?
3. What is a statistically significant (average, mode, etc.) timing?

```
 1   PROGRAM unorderedsearch ( input, output );
 2
 3   TYPE
 4       anarray = ARRAY [1..1000] OF integer;
 5
 6   FUNCTION noorder ( value : anarray;
 7                        size : integer;
 8                        item : integer ) : integer;
 9
10       VAR
11          i : integer;
12
13       BEGIN
14       i := size;
15       WHILE ( i > 0 ) AND ( item <> value [i] )  DO
16           i := i - 1;
17       noorder := i
18       END;   { RETURNS 0 IF value NOT FOUND }
```

Figure 10.1.   Search Procedure for an Unordered Array

```
 1   PROGRAM orderedsearch ( input, output );
 2
 3   TYPE
 4       anarray = ARRAY [1..1000] OF integer;
 5
 6   FUNCTION ordered ( value : anarray;
 7                        size, item : integer ) : integer;
 8
 9       VAR
10          i : integer;
11
12       BEGIN
13       i := 1;
14       WHILE ( i <= size ) AND ( item > value [i]   ) DO
15           i := i + 1;
16       ordered := i
17       END;    { RETURNS POSSIBLE LOCATION WHEN value NOT FOUND }
```

Figure 10.2.   Search Procedure for an Ordered Array

Considering the worst and statistically significant time is complicated by another consideration, namely:

4. What happens to the timing if ITEM is not in the array?

```
1    PROGRAM unorderedupdate ( input, output );
2
3    TYPE
4        anarray = ARRAY [1..1000] OF integer;
5
6    PROCEDURE update1 ( VAR value : anarray;
7                        VAR size : integer;
8                        item : integer );
9
10       BEGIN
11       size := size + 1;   value [size] := item
12       END;
```

Figure 10.3.   Update for an Unordered Array

```
1    PROGRAM orderedupdate ( input, output );
2
3    TYPE
4        anarray = ARRAY [1..1000] OF integer;
5
6    PROCEDURE update2 ( VAR value : anarray;
7                        VAR size : integer;
8                        item : integer );
9
10       VAR
11           start, i : integer;
12
13       BEGIN
14       start := ordered (value, size, item);    size := size + 1;
15       FOR i := size DOWNTO start+1 DO
16           value [i] := value [i-1];
17       value [start] := item
18       END;
```

Figure 10.4.   Update for an Ordered Array

Because of this fourth consideration, the first three are evaluated assuming the value in ITEM is in the array. Under this assumption, the best case, worst case, and average timings are the same, namely, O(1), O(N), O(N/2), respectively. One can arrive at an average time of O(N/2) by observing that if it is equally likely that item is any one of the N items, then the probability of ITEM being at location I is 1/N. Therefore the expected value is

$$1 * 1/N + 2 * 1/N + \ldots + N * 1/N = O(N/2).$$

However when the value in ITEM is not in the array, the program in figure 10.1 executes in time O(N). This is because each value in the array must be tested. However, the program in figure 10.2 assumes the array is in order. If

$$A(1) \leq ITEM \leq A(N)$$

then, on the average the timing is O(N/2).

```
1    PROGRAM bisectionsearch ( input, output );
2
3    TYPE
4        anarray = ARRAY [1..1000] OF integer;
5
6    FUNCTION bisection ( value : anarray;
7                         size : integer;
8                         item : integer ) : integer;
9
10       VAR
11           low, high, mid : integer;
12
13       BEGIN
14       low := 1;   high := size + 1;   mid := (low+high) DIV 2;
15       WHILE ( low <> mid ) AND ( item <> value [mid] ) DO
16           BEGIN
17           IF item < value [mid] THEN
18               high := mid
19           ELSE
20               low := mid;
21           mid := (low + high) DIV 2
22           END;
23       IF item <> value [mid] THEN
24           bisection := mid + 1
25       ELSE
26           bisection := mid
27       END;  { RETURNS POSSIBLE LOCATION IF value NOT FOUND }
```

Figure 10.5. Bisection Search Procedure

The search time advantage gained by ordering the array appears to be lost when the array is updated. An unsorted array is updated simply by placing the new item in the next available position, N+1, and resetting the indicated size of the array, see figure 10.3. This update time is constant. On the other hand, to update an ordered array, once the position for the new item is found (which takes time), room must be made by moving every item down one location, item I goes to position I+1, starting at the location where the new item is to be placed, down to the end of the collection. On the average, this takes N/2 loop iterations, see figure 10.4.

10:2. Bisection Method Search

Given an ordered collection of data, figure 10.5 illustrates a better search method, called bisection. This method takes advantage of the order of the data by setting up two indices, LOW and HIGH, then bisecting their range. A comparison determines the relationship between the item being searched for and the midpoint of the range indicated by LOW and HIGH. If the item is found, the search terminates, otherwise, either LOW or HIGH is reset to indicate the reduced range of values that must contain the item.

For example, if we are searching through the array in figure 10.6 for the number 17, the first time through the outer loop of the program in 10.5, 17 < 45. Therefore, HIGH is reset to MID. The second time through the WHILE loop, 12 is compared to 17. Since 17 > 12, LOW is reset. The next time through the loop, the number is found.

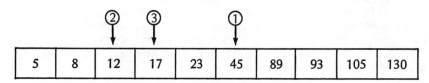

| 5 | 8 | 12 | 17 | 23 | 45 | 89 | 93 | 105 | 130 |

Figure 10.6.   Illustration of bisection procedure

Each time through the loop, the range is cut in half. Therefore, the number of loop iterations required to find an item is

$$LOG_2 \quad N.$$

This is a dramatic improvement over the sequential search timing. To see how important this is, an array of 1,000,000 items could not be sequentially searched, on the average, in a reasonable amount of time. But a bisection search would find an item in at most 20 loop iterations, log 1000000.

One quick observation about the algorithm is that the variable HIGH is initially set to SIZE+1. This at first might look like an error. However, this is done to eliminate the truncation that occurs when the middle value is computed. Because of this, if the item that is being searched for was in the last position of the array, the procedure would not find it because of the truncation that occurs and accumulates with the calculation

$$MID = (LOW + HIGH) \; DIV \; 2.$$

See the exercises for more about this problem.

The bisection method, although a dramatic improvement in search time, is still confronted with O(N) update time. For an array of items with few updates, this would not be a problem. But, if substantial updating would occur, there could be some time problems.

10:3. Direct Address Search and Update

The ideal search and update situation would be when both searching and updating take a constant amount of time. In searching for that ideal, one might be willing to consider some reasonable compromises, specifically:

1. The range of potential values is known;
2. The distribution of values in the range will approximate some known distribution;
3. There is considerably more memory space available for the data than the actual amount of data that will be processed.

Consider a case with the following assumptions: All data is in the range from -10000 to 10000, and is uniformly distributed in that range. Only about 1000 items are expected to be processed, but an array of 3000 locations is available. Uniformly distributed means that the numbers that occur are scattered in the range so that the probability of any number occurring is about the same, namely one over the range.

One method of handling this situation is an address calculation procedure. In general this procedure uses an address function which takes the value in question and computes the address of the location in the array where the number is expected to be placed or to appear. Under the assumptions of the previous paragraph, the address calculation function would be a linear function that relates the range of possible values to the indices that are available,

$$\text{ADDRESS} = \text{INT} \left(\frac{\text{SIZE}}{\text{RANGE}} (\text{VALUE} - \text{MIN}) + 1 \right).$$

Naturally, there is the possibility that two numbers will compute the same array address. This possibility is minimized when the data is very close to being uniformly distributed in the range and by using an array that is substantially larger than the number of values anticipated.

One problem with the address calculation approach is recognizing an empty array location. This is taken care of by initializing all the array postions with a value that is outside of the range. This initialization takes time O(size of the array) and hence it could be of some concern if the array is substantially large.

A second difficulty with an address calculation procedure is the possibility of two different values computing the same array address. This possibility affects the timing of both the search and update processes. Figure 10.7 illustrates an address calculation search. The index computation should calculate

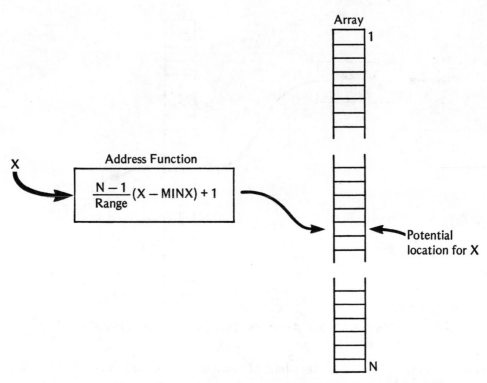

Figure 10.7.   Address Calculation Procedure

the actual location of the value.   If not, the procedure searches sequentially in the appropriate direction until either the value is found or the potential location of the value is found.

The update procedure has an additional complication.   The procedure must also make sure it stays within the bounds of the array while searching for an available space.   Because of this procedure and the possibility of two values producing the same address, the desired constant time will not be achieved. Once an empty space is found, the items in the array between the calculated address and the available space must be moved so that the new item can be inserted and the values maintained in their proper order.   Since the available space might be either before or after the address calculated index, the algorithm must be able to move items in either direction in the array and insert the new item so that all the data is in order.   This is left as an exercise.

Several address calculation experiments are suggested in the exercise section. One variation uses linked lists.   In this case, the address calculation locates a pointer in an array of pointers, then all the values that have produced that

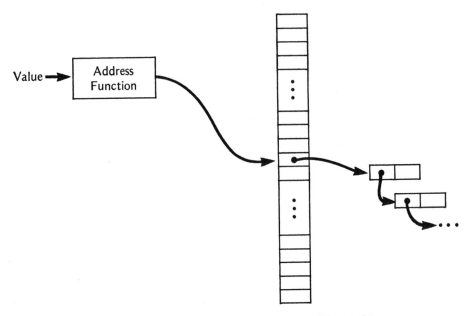

Figure 10.8.   Address Calculation with Linking

pointer's index appear in the list of values whose list head is that pointer (see figure 10.8).

10:4. Hashing

Not all searching and update problems involve numbers. Many use keys that are strings of characters. A popular method of searching and updating sets of strings in a time efficient manner is a variation of the approach described in section 10:3. In search and update problems, it is not always necessary for the item to be in some collating order. The important criteria are that items are included or found in a time efficient manner.

This approach is called hashing. Like address calculation, the item is used in a calculation scheme that computes an index into a pointer array. The calculation can be any manipulation of the bit patterns of the characters in the string. For example, the bit patterns can be added, shifted, etc., then the result divided by the size of the pointer array and the remainder of the division used as an index into the pointer array.

There are no limits to the possible number of hashing functions. The only criteria are that the function be time efficient, that all possible indices can be computed by the function, and that the function produces all indices in some uniform way. That is, the hashing function should not have a bias that produces certain indices substantially more than others. If it does, the search and update timings are adversely affected.

Hashing is an alternative to the dictionary tree approach to keeping strings of characters. However, the dictionary tree can produce a collated concordance of the strings in the tree. But the timing for accessing in a hashing scheme is normally better than the timing for a dictionary tree. There are several tradeoffs that must be considered when weighing a choice between hashing and other methods, like a dictionary tree. In general, hashing is fast, as long as the hashing function is compatible with the data being hashed, and its memory utilization is very good.

10:5. Block Sequential Search and Update

Sequential searching is popular because of the ease with which it can be programmed and the very small amount of space consumed by the code. Unfortunately it has the poorest search time of the methods described in this chapter. The following modification of the search procedure improves search time.

As in the case of address calculation, assume the range of potential values is known. If something is known about the potential distribution of values then that information is used to initialize the array, otherwise the initialization is performed assuming the potential values are uniformly distributed in the array. With this method, the array is viewed as blocks of locations. Let B be the size of each block, if N is the array size, then there are Int (N/B) or Int (N/B)+1 blocks.

The first location in each block is initialized with a representative value for that block and the second location in each block is initialized with a value outside of the range to indicate that the rest of the block is empty. For example, if the range of values was 0 through 100000, the values uniformly distributed in that range, the array has 1000 values, and b is 50, then the initialization procedure could place 0,2000,4000, etc. in array locations 1,21,41,etc. Also, a value outside of the range, for example, -1, is placed in locations 2,22,42,etc. This initialization is performed assuming that the values will be uniformly distributed in the range.

Now the update and search procedures find the possible location of a value by using a procedure like the one described in figure 10.9. This procedure first searches for the block that could potentially contain the value, then the procedure does a sequential search through that block. At this point, the search procedure determines if the value is in the array. The update procedure determines if there is space available in the block and, if so, updates the block. If space is not available within the block, then there are various options that can be carried out (see the exercises).

```
 1   PROGRAM blocksequential ( input, output );
 2
 3   TYPE
 4       anarray = ARRAY [1..1000] OF integer
 5
 6   FUNCTION blocked ( value : anarray;
 7                      size, item : integer ) : integer;
 8
 9       CONST
10           blocksize = 25;
11
12       VAR
13           incr, i : integer;
14
15       BEGIN
16       incr := blocksize; i := 1;
17       WHILE incr <> 0 DO
18           BEGIN
19           WHILE ( i <= size ) AND ( item < value[i] ) DO
20               i := i + incr;
21           IF item = value[i] THEN
22               incr := 0
23           ELSE
24               BEGIN
25               i := i - incr;
26               incr := incr DIV blocksize
27               END
28           END
29       END;  { blocked RETURNS THE POTENTIAL POSITION OF value }
30             {   CONTINUED ON THE NEXT PAGE  }
```

The maximum time for the procedure in figure 10.9 is easy to obtain. With B blocks, it takes at most B loop iterations to find the block and N/B loop iterations to find the value in the block. This produces a time result of $O(B+N/B)$. This leads to a question of the existence of an ideal blocksize. The ideal blocksize would produce a minimum value for

$$T = B + N/B.$$

Once again, returning to calculus, a function takes on a minimum value at points where the first derivative is zero and the second derivative is positive. For a fixed array of size N, taking the first and second derivatives yields

$$T' = 1 - N/B^2$$

and

```
31    PROCEDURE update4 ( VAR value : anarray;
32                        size, item : integer );
33
34       CONST
35          empty = 2000000000;
36
37       VAR
38          place, i, extra : integer;
39
40       BEGIN
41       place := blocked (value, size, item);
42       i := item;
43       WHILE ( place <= size ) AND ( value[place] <> empty ) DO
44          BEGIN
45          extra := value[place];   value[place] := i;
46          i := extra;    place := place + 1
47          END;
48       IF place <= size THEN
49          value[place] := i
50       ELSE
51          writeln (' LAST BLOCK FILLED')
52       END;
```

Figure 10.9.   Block Sequential Search Algorithm

$$T'' = 2N/B^3.$$

Setting T' = 0 yields the ideal blocksize of SQRT(B), or the integer value closest to that. Specifically, for the example above, this would mean that the blocksize of 50 was not a very good choice. Better blocksizes would be near SORT(1000), that is 33 or 34.

10:6. Observations

Search and update methods form the nucleus of several important techniques that are used to store and maintain information on disks and other pseudo-random access devices. The block sequential search is analogous to the indexed sequential access method. The AVL tree, described in chapter 8, is the basis of many pseudorandom file structure methods based on B* trees. In both cases, the timing information would be relevant, but it would have to be modified to take into account the functional characteristics of the device containing the information.

To illustrate, consider the case of B-trees implemented on disks. Assume that 4096 bytes can be conveniently accessed from a disk during one read operation. One operating system allocates B-tree files by starting with two 4K units. In one of them it starts to store the data sequentially. In the other, a B-tree is created. As more space is needed for the tree or the data, additional units of disk space are allocated. The advantage of B-tree storage is that with only two or three 4K units of disk space, a tree can be created for a very large file. In addition, any record in the file can be accessed in three or four disk accesses, two or three accesses to the tree, and one access to the disk unit to get to the data. Since a disk access is a real time consuming operation, the B-tree is a real asset because it limits the number of disk accesses required to access one record.

10:7. EXERCISES

1. Verify the best case, worst case, and average timings for the programs in figures 10.1 and 10.2.

2. Step through a bisection method example searching for the occurrence of ITEM where the ITEM is in the last array location, A(SIZE). Do this twice, once with HIGH=SIZE and once with HIGH=SIZE+1.

3. The address calculation function described in section 10.3 will allow only one value to compute the maximum array index. Make a simple modification that will more uniformly use all array locations, specifically, the last array location.

4. Write and test address calculation search and update procedures. Test these procedures with various sized collections of numbers and various sized arrays. In particular, for a given size collection of numbers, how does the number of loop iterations vary as the array size changes?

5. Write and test procedures for the linked list variations of the address calculation search and update.

6. Determine an address calculation procedure for a normally distributed set of numbers.

7. Evaluate a hashing scheme which adds the bit patterns of the characters and uses the remainder when divided by the pointer array size as the index into the array.

8. Make a detailed comparison of the space costs of a dictionary tree and a hashing scheme for maintaining character strings.

9. Write an update algorithm for the blocked sequential search. Have your procedure handle block overflow, by finding space in a neighboring block. Time your algorithm.

10. Read the literature on ISAM files and evaluate the various overflow methods. What makes the block sequential approach of ISAM valuable for organizing files on pseudorandom access devices?

11

Recursion

Recursion is a mathematical concept and a valuable programming methodology. Unfortunately, not all programming languages support recursion. For that reason, it is presented in this chapter as a self contained unit and is not emphasized elsewhere in this text. This chapter includes some ideas on how to recognize when recursion might be an appropriate programming technique. The exercise section suggests several recursive programming assignments.

11:1. Intuition and Mathematics

Many times, a mathematician might define a concept in terms of itself. For example, the factorial function, n!, can be defined as

$$n! = n * (n-1)! \text{ when } n > 0,$$
$$= 1 \text{ when } n = 0.$$

Here, the definition of factorial contains a reference to itself. However, the definition makes sense in that it does eventually terminate with an answer,

$$5! = 5 * 4! = 5 * 4 * 3! = 5 * 4 * 3 * 2!$$
$$= 5 * 4 * 3 * 2 * 1! = 120 * 0! = 120.$$

This is an example of a recursive definition.

Another example is the product rule for differentiation,

$$\frac{d(f(x) * g(x))}{d x} = \frac{d f(x)}{d x} * g(x) + f(x) * \frac{d g(x)}{d x}.$$

Here, the product rule for differentiation is defined in terms of all the rules for differentiation. Because of the rules for differentiation, the process does eventually terminate with an answer.

```
1   PROGRAM factorial ( input, output );
2
3   FUNCTION factorial ( n : integer ): integer;
4
5      VAR
6         nless1 : integer
7
8      BEGIN
9      IF n > 0 THEN
10         BEGIN
11         nless1 := n - 1;
12         factorial := n * factorial( nless1 )
13         END
14      ELSE
15         factorial := 1
16      END;
```

Figure 11.1. A Recursive n! Procedure

Some programming languages support a recursive capability which allows programmers to define procedures or functions that can directly or indirectly call
themselves.   Figure 11.1 contains a PASCAL program that defines a factorial
function.   Note that the IF-ELSE clause in the function yields a direct interpretation of the recursive definition of factorial.

11:2. Fundamentals of Recursive Programming

An easy way to think of how recursion is implemented is to consider the existence of multiple copies of the variables that are defined in a recursive procedure.   For example, in the factorial function in figure 11.1, each time the
procedure calls itself, a new copy of the variable 'nless1' is created along
with the proper linkage so that the program can execute the procedure and
properly terminate execution.

The factorial procedure in figure 11.1 is a classical example of recursion, but
not a good example of how recursion should be used.   This is because there
are other ways of writing a factorial procedure without using recursion.   A
better illustration of the use of recursion appears in figure 11.2.   This is another quicksort algorithm.   However, if you compare it to the quicksort algorithm that appears in chapter 4, figure 4.6., the first observation one should
make is that it contains less code.   The reason for this is that the pushdown
stacks have disappeared.   Note that the quicksort procedure now has three
arguments, a, min, and n. The new argument, min, along with n indicate to
the procedure which part of the array a is to be sorted.   Therefore, the initial call to the procedure quick would pass the value 1 in the parameter 'min'
and the size of the array in 'n'.   Initially, the procedure would start sorting

```
1   PROGRAM quicksort (input, output);
2
3   TYPE
4      anarray = ARRAY [ 1..5000 ] OF integer;
5
6   PROCEDURE quick ( VAR a: anarray;
7                     low, high: integer);
8
9      TYPE
10        dset = (up, down);
11
12     VAR
13        direction: dset;
14        top, key, lowup, highdown: integer;
15
16     BEGIN { of quick }
17         IF low < high THEN
18             BEGIN
19             lowup := low;  highdown := high;
20             direction := down;  key := a [low];
21             WHILE lowup <> highdown DO
22                BEGIN
23                IF direction = down THEN
24                    IF key < a [highdown] THEN
25                        highdown := highdown - 1
26                    ELSE BEGIN
27                        a [lowup] := a [highdown];
28                        direction := up
29                        END
30                ELSE
31                    IF key > a [lowup] THEN
32                        lowup := lowup + 1
33                    ELSE BEGIN
34                        a [highdown] := a [lowup];
35                        direction := down
36                        END
37                END;
38             IF (high  - highdown) > (lowup - low) THEN
39                BEGIN
40                quick ( a, low, lowup - 1);
41                quick ( a, highdown + 1, high)
42                END
43             ELSE
44                BEGIN
45                quick ( a, highdown + 1, high);
46                quick ( a, low, lowup - 1)
47                END
48             END
49     END { of quick }
```

Figure 11.2. A Recursive Quicksort

the whole array as it did for the program in figure 4.6. However, rather than pushing two sets of values into the two pushdown stacks of figure 4.6, the procedure recursively calls itself. When the procedure calls itself, the current status of all local variables is saved and new locations are allocated for the local variables. Also, any parameters that are not VARed, that is, any parameters that are not used for returning values, are also reallocated and the old copies of these variables are saved, 'min' and 'n'. Each time the procedure recursively calls itself, these actions occur. When the procedure terminates, the copies of the last set of local variables are resorted and the procedure continues executing immediately after the recursive call to itself.

The quicksort algorithm is typical of a good use of recursion. Any recursive procedure can always be written without recursion, but not always conveniently. Therefore, to some extent, recursion is a programming frill. However, when it can help present a high level description of an algorithm and to avoid some implementational details, then is an excellent approach.

How does one recognize when recursion is an appropriate technique? There are normally two possible clues. The first one is the obvious situation where an algorithm is recursively defined, either directly or indirectly. The second is the use of a stack structure as in figure 4.6. The stacks in figure 4.6 store the intermediate status as the quicksort executes. That is, the stacks indicate those parts of the array that still must be sorted. This is precisely what the recursive call to the procedure do, namely, keep the status of those parts of the array that still must be sorted. In a sense, we could say that the quicksort of figure 4.6 was driven, or guided by the pushdown stacks. Any time an algorithm uses a pushdown stack in this way to control itself, the algorithm is a prime candidate for recursion. This is typified by the use of recursion in many microcomputer operating systems.

11:3. Performing Recursion

The relation between stacks and recursion is not coincidental. When a recursive program executes, pushdown stacks save the current status of the procedure and allocate the new local variables. As the procedure executes, each time a recursive call occurs, the current status of all the variables as well as where the call was made in the program is stored in a pushdown stack and the new copies of the variables are allocated in the same stack. When a recursive call terminates, the copies of its local variables are popped from the stack, then the information about where the call was made is also released from the stack so that the program can continue on where it had left off when the recursive call was made.

The precise details of how this is carried out vary somewhat from language to language and to some extent depend upon the hardware capabilities that support stack architecture in a computer. These details are best left for another course. In general, one should be cautious about using recursion extensively because hidden in its implementation can be large time and space costs. However, most PASCAL systems are reasonably efficient when it comes to recursion.

Figure 11.3 illustrates a recursive procedure that prints the words placed in a dictionary tree, see chapter 7. The words are printed in alphabetical order. The procedure is based upon the natural order tree search illustrated in figure 7.14.

11:4. EXERCISES

1. Write a recursive procedure to perform a natural order tree search.

2. Write a recursive procedure to evaluate Reverse Polish Expressions.

3. Write a recursive procedure to generate Fibonacci numbers.

4. Find other recursive mathematical definitions and formulas and determine whether recursion is an appropriate method of carrying them out.

5. Write programs to recursively carry out the appropriate procedures you found in exercise 4.

```
 1    PROGRAM alphabetized (input, output);
 2
 3    TYPE
 4       anarray = PACKED ARRAY [ 1..50 ] OF char;
 5       tpoint = ↑treerecord;
 6       treerecord = RECORD
 7                          child, sibling: tpoint;
 8                          letter: char;
 9                          endword: boolean;
10                       END;
11
12    VAR
13       root: tpoint;
14       word: anarray;
15       size: integer;
16
17    PROCEDURE wordlist (node: tpoint;
18                        VAR word: anarray;
19                        VAR n: integer);
20
21       VAR i: integer
22
23       BEGIN
24       n := succ (n);
25       word [n] := node↑.letter;
26       IF node↑.child <> NIL
27          THEN wordlist (node↑.child, word, n);
28       IF node↑.endword
29          THEN BEGIN
30             FOR i := 1 TO n DO write (output, word [i]);
31             writeln (output)
32             END;
33       n := pred (n);
34       IF node↑sibling <> NIL
35          THEN wordlist (node↑.sibling, word, n)
36       END;
38
39    { other procedures here }
40
41    BEGIN
42
43    { code to build tree here }
44
45    size := 0;
46    wordlist (root, word, size);
47
48    END.
```

Figure 11.3. A Recursive printing of a dictionary tree

12

Storage Allocation

Dynamic allocation can be a very useful capability. Up to this point it was assumed that it was available and that its time and space costs were nomimal. But are they? There are many ways to perform dynamic allocation. Here two general approaches are presented, one where a list of available space is maintained, and another called garbage collection. Several variations of the list approach are described and the basic differences in philosophy between these two approaches are discussed. There is still much work to be done in dynamic allocation. All the approaches can be made to fail, or consume great amounts of time. An approach is said to fail if there is sufficient space to meet a request for space but the space has not been properly organized to satisfy the request.

12:1. Dynamic Allocation - Concepts

There are many different approaches to handling unused storage so that it can be allocated as required. This is very important to most operating systems because various storage allocation techniques manage the peripheral storage space (disks, drums, etc.) as well as managing primary memory in a multiprogramming environment. This must be done so that each user obtains the space he needs and does not interfere with other users.

There are two general approaches to storage management. One of these groups of techniques keeps the available storage in some order while the other approach does not. In the second approach, either the storage being used or that not being used is marked in some way so that it can be recognized. Most approaches, regardless of which group they are in, use some organization of the available space, or at least part of it. Typically, when the available space is organized, it is put into a list where each record in the list is an available piece of storage and contains information about its size as well as a pointer to the next available piece of storage.

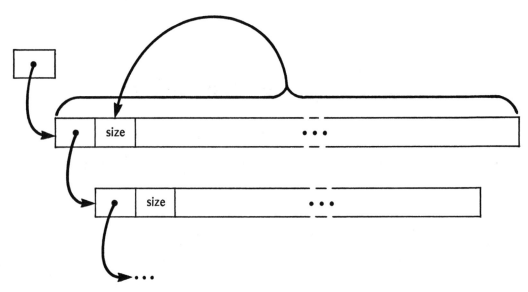

Figure 12.1. A LAVS illustration

The storage allocation procedures are described using their PASCAL names NEW, to obtain space, and DISPOSE, to release space. A key towards distinguishing between the two groupings is the way PASCAL's DISPOSE can perform. In just about all cases, the NEW procedure is about the same, namely, it searches through a list of available space looking for a record that is big enough to satisfy the request, and removes that record or at least part of it from the list to satisfy the request. Therefore, the cost of the NEW operation is usually at most equal to

O(Number of records in the list of available space) .

DISPOSE on the other hand usually maintains the organization of the list of available space, or simple marks or unmarks records that are returned. In the approaches described below, the timing of DISPOSE ranges between being simply a constant amount of time to time linearly bound by the number of records in the list of available space.

12:2. List of Available Space

Most approaches to dynamic storage allocation maintain a **List of Available Space, LAVS.** Typically, this approach begins by organizing the available space as if the space is one large dynamic record. As requests are made for space, the requested space is cut from that one large record. In the approaches discussed in this section, as space is released through DISPOSE requests, it is linked to the other available space so that eventually, the available space forms a list as illustrated in figure 12.1. This means that NEW must be smart enough to search through this list and find dynamic records of a sufficient size to meet each request. If the record it finds is larger than requested, NEW breaks a record into two pieces and returns the unused part to the LAVS.

> SET a pointer to the beginning of the LAVS
> WHILE the record pointed to is not large enough
>   follow the pointer in a record to the next record
> IF there is too much space in the record
>   break the record in two parts and
>   return the unused part to the LAVS
> set the NEW pointer to the record that was removed.

Figure 12.2. A NEW Algorithm

Figure 12.2 illustrates a NEW algorithm which works with two of the three dynamic allocation schemes described in this section. This procedure searches through the LAVS until it finds a record of sufficient size to meet the request for space, the record is unlinked and if the record is larger than needed to meet the request, then the unused portion is relinked into the LAVS. Note that the unused portion is relinked into the LAVS only if it contains two or more locations. This is because each record in the LAVS needs at least two locations, one as a link and the other to indicate the size of the record.

The three methods of organizing the LAVS that are described here can be delineated by how DISPOSE operates. These three methods are referred to as:

1. The stack approach - The last record returned is at the top of the stack (the beginning of the list);
2. Organization by-size - The records in LAVS are kept in collating order (smallest to largest, or largest to smallest);
3. Organization by-location - The records in LAVS are kept in order of their actual memory addresses, smallest to largest.

In the stack approach, DISPOSE simply performs like the PUSH operation for a pushdown stack kept as a list. As such, it is very time efficient because it performs within a constant amount of time. The second approach, by-size, requires that DISPOSE search the LAVS and find the position in LAVS where the returned record should be placed so that the LAVS can maintain its organization. Naturally, this DISPOSE operation takes more time than the stack approach. But if that time is spent organizing the LAVS and the organization can be exploited, then the extra time for the second approach might be worth it.

In the second approach, there are two possible collating orders, ascending order of record size or descending order of record size. There are some tradeoffs between these two that should be considered. A LAVS kept in descending order could respond more rapidly to requests for larger records than if the LAVS is kept in ascending order of record size. However, if kept in descending order, when requests for smaller records are made, either larger records would be cut into smaller ones although smaller ones might be in the LAVS, or more time would have to be spent searching the LAVS to obtain the smallest record that could satisfy the request.

It is important to understand that it is not desirable to break larger records into smaller ones to satisfy requests when smaller records are available to meet the request. This atrophy is undesirable. As a program executes, the records available in the LAVS become smaller. Eventually, the approach can fail because there is sufficient space to meet a request but the space is in the wrong form, namely, a list of very small records.

There are methods of slowing down the atrophy when the LAVS is kept in descending order of size. For comparison against other approaches, assume that the LAVS by-size approach keeps the records in ascending order. This will guarantee that large records are not broken into smaller records when records of sufficient size are not available to handle a NEW request.

assume 100 locations originally in LAVS

NEW(50) - both allocations would now have one record of 50
NEW(20) - both allocations would now have one record of 30
DISPOSE(20) - stack now 20-30, by-size now 20-30
DISPOSE(50) - stack now 50-20-30, by-size now 20-30-50
NEW(20) - stack now 30-20-30, by-size now 30-50
NEW(50) - stack cannot fill request, by-size has one record of 30

Figure 12.3. By-size allocation succeeds, stack allocation fails

Consider the sequence of requests for space described in figure 12.3. After the first four calls, the by-size approach would have the LAVS in the order 20-30-50 while the stack approach would have the LAVS ordered 50-20-30. The fifth statement would produce a LAVS of 30-50 in the "by-size" organization and 30-20-30 in the stack organization. As a result, the last request, NEW(50) cannot be filled by the stack organization and hence the allocation procedure fails.

The sequence of calls in figure 12.4 illustrates a case where by-size allocation fails and stack allocation succeeds. In this case, the stack allocation, by coassume the LAVS originally contains 100 locations.

NEW(30) - both allocations would now have one record of 70
NEW(20) - both allocations would now have one record of 50
NEW(50) - both allocations have no space left
DISPOSE(20) - both have one record of 20
DISPOSE(30) - stack now 30-20, by-size now 20-30
NEW(15) - stack now 15-20, by-size now 5-30
NEW(15) - stack now has one record of 20, by-size now 5-15
NEW(20) - stack allocation fills request, by-size fails

Figure 12.4.   Stack allocation succeeds, by-size allocation fails

incidence, organizes the available space in such a way that a record of the right size just happens to be divided. The by-size allocation causes the record of size 20 to be cut into two pieces, one of which is too small to satisfy later requests.

The cause of failure of the by-size approach in this example is a typical cause of failure of most dynamic allocation schemes, namely, atrophy. That is, the available space has been fragmented into small records which cannot satisfy the requests for space. Another method attempts to put small records back together and reconstruct them into larger records. But records can be combined to form larger records only if they are physically contiguous. There is a third LAVS approach that does this. It keeps records in the LAVS by-location.

In the by-location approach, the LAVS is organized in ascending or descending order of the memory addresses of the pointers in the LAVS. Assume that ascending order of pointer address values is chosen. Since each record also contains its size, the DISPOSE routine can recognize when two records are physically beside each other. This can be done by simply observing when the address of the beginning of one record (the pointer to that record) plus the size of the record equals the address of the other record. When this is observed, the two records can be joined together to form one larger record.

assume 100 locations originally in LAVS

10 requests for NEW(10) - all space used by all methods
10 returns of space through DISPOSE(10)
                by-location has 1 record of 100
                by-size and stack organization have 10 records of 10
NEW(20) - By-location succeeds, other two methods fail.

Figure 12.5.   By-Location allocation succeeds, others fail

Figure 12.5 illustrates a sequence of calls in which the by-location approach succeeds and the other two methods fail. They fail because they do not construct larger records from smaller ones. This should not be interpreted as a wholesale endorsement of the by-location approach over the other two. On the contrary, examples can be constructed in which each of the other two methods succeed and the by-location approach fails! Construction of this example is given as an exercise. However, a variation of the case described in figure 12.4 can be constructed to make by-size succeed and the other two methods fail.

This creates a real dilemma. Since examples can be constructed to make any one method look good and the others look bad, what are we to do? There are two answers, neither of which are ideal. First, the examples that were constructed are rare, but similar cases can occur. Normally, the amount of memory available for dynamic allocation is so large that only when its limits are pushed do problems occur. So, for many different programming problems, any method for performing dynamic allocation would work. Second, and this is a personal bias, the by-location method does at least combat some of the atrophy that can occur in the other two methods. Therefore, with many programming problems, if it fails, chances are the other two methods would also fail.

The methods described here as ways of managing the memory with the NEW and DISPOSE procedures are analogous to methods used by operating systems to manage disc storage allocation. The problems of allocating space as files are being created, modified, and deleted are compounded by the characteristics of the storage medium. Variations of these methods are used to allocate disk space. These variations go beyond the scope of this text.

12:3. Mark/Release

PASCAL allocates local variables in procedures as the procedures are entered. Local variables are released when the procedure terminates. This is accomplished by manipulating the available space as if it was a pushdown stack. Many versions of PASCAL compilers for minicomputers and microcomputers provide users with control over dynamically allocated space by allowing users to manipulate it as if it was also allocated as a stack.

Typically, this is accomplished through two procedures called **mark** and **release**. This approach is not appropriate for all programs that use dynamic allocation. However, there is a large collection of problems for which this approach does work. Any program which satisfies the following criterion can use **mark** and **release**: If a pair of positions in the program's execution can be determined such that any space allocated after the first position and before the second position is no longer used after the second point. In this case, a pointer variable is set,

mark(p),

at the first position.   Then, at the second position in the program, place

release(p).

The result is that the dynamically allocated space that was manipulated between the calls to mark and release are restored to their status as it was at
the position when mark was performed.   Mark and release may appear many
times in a program and with as many different pointer variables as desired.
The only requirement is that the variables must be allocated as pointer variables and they should not be modified by a program between their appear-
ances in mark and release.

If several variables are being used by mark and release to control dynamic
storage allocation, then there are some simple rules that should be followed to
avoid problems.   For any two pointers, say p and q, their uses in pairs of
marks and releases must either be disjoint or nested.   A disjoint use would
be when mark(p) and release(p) appear before mark(q).   A nested use would
be if mark(p) is followed by mark(q) before release(p) occurs.   This is a
nested case and release(q) must appear before release(p).

In general, dynamic allocation is a very sophisticated use of the resources of
a computer.   It should be done with great care and good programming methods are essential.   Good top down stepwise development of programs is a must
because debugging poorly designed programs that use dynamic allocation is
extremely difficult.

12:4. Garbage Collection

An alternate and widely used approach to space management is called **garbage
collection**.   In this method, the DISPOSE algorithm does not place unused records back into the LAVS.   Rather, this approach waits until the LAVS is
depleted, then it "collects garbage".   That is, it determines which space is
not used and makes it available again.   To do this, the garbage collection algorithm must know where the various structures are located.   This means
that it must have access to a program's data structures and know how the
data structures are linked so that they can be traversed and the space
marked.   Then the unmarked space is organized into a new LAVS.

The garbage collection algorithm must have some way of traversing all of a
program's structures and mark them so that unused space can be distin-
guished from the existing structures.   Here is the catch.   Garbage collection
is done only when no more space is available.   Where does the garbage collection algorithm get the space to mark used records?   Where does it get the intermediate storage space that it needs to search through complex data structures?   The answer is, it doesn't!

If garbage collection is performed, the records that are allocated usually contain some space which can only be accessed by the garbage collection algorithm. This is a very small amount of space, perhaps only a bit per unit of memory. The garbage collection algorithm can turn these bits on and off to indicate whether or not a memory location is in a structure. That is all the space needed by the garbage collection to mark the memory. But what about the auxiliary space needed by the garbage collection algorithm to traverse trees and other structures? There is no space available for a pushdown stack. With no space available, the garbage collection algorithm must function in a way similar to the procedure described in figure 12.6.

```
mark all space as unused
FOR each structure
:   SCAN the structure and mark its nodes.
END FOR LOOP
collect all unmarked memory into a new LAVS
end of algorithm
```

```
                SCAN

DO UNTIL THE ROOT NODE IS MARKED
:   SET A POINTER TO THE ROOT
:   DO UNTIL THE POINTER INDICATES A MARKED LOCATION
:   :   IF THE LEFT CHILD IS NOT MARKED
:   :       RESET THE POINTER TO THE LEFT CHILD
:   :   ELSEIF RIGHT CHILD EXISTS AND IS NOT MARKED
:   :       RESET POINTER TO THE RIGHT CHILD
:   :   ELSE
:   :       MARK THE LOCATIONS IN THIS RECORD
:   :   ENDIF
:   ENDDO
ENDDO
```

Figure 12.6. Tree scan procedure for garbage collection

Figure 12.6 illustrates two algorithms. The first is the general scheme for garbage collection and the second illustrates a natural order tree marking algorithm which does not use an auxiliary storage. One look at the timing of this algorithm and the difficulties are immediately apparent. Suppose the tree marking is done on a very unbalanced tree. That is, suppose the tree has $O(n)$ nodes and $O(n)$ is also the length of at least one path in the tree. Then the time of the algorithm could be bound by

$$O(\ n^n).$$

This is not very desirable. However, this is not a good reason to discard garbage collection. Remember, cases were constructed to make each of the other techniques fail. If the space needed by an algorithm is there and it is contiguous, the garbage collection succeeds, most of the time. It can be made to fail just like the others failed. Also, the reasons for failure in the other cases were because the DISPOSE algorithm returned space to LAVS and its LAVS organization failed. Garbage collection does not use DISPOSE in this way, therefore, it cannot fail in the same way that the others failed.

12:5. Dynamic Allocation - Current Hardware/Software Trends

As the size of both the main and peripheral storage on computers increases, what will be the effect of this on dynamic allocation? New hardware with its paging and virtual memory capabilities also has an effect on the efficiency of and need for dynamic allocation. More memory and more peripheral storage mean that storage allocation routines have more to manage. Therefore their efficiency and correctness become even more important. This becomes very obvious if one looks at the current literature.

As computers are used to tackle more and more sophisticated problems, there is more demand for more sophisticated data structuring techniques, including the use of dynamic allocation. As computer systems, even mini-computers, become larger, they too demand correct and efficient storage management.

More advanced operating systems and hardware do not eliminate storage management. Rather, they control it for users in a way that is transparent to most users. But it's still there, and being aware of it and how it works can help make programs more efficient and effective.

12:6. EXERCISES

1. Write a NEW algorithm which searches LAVS and uses the most appropriate record to fulfill a request for space, that is, a record of the exact size, or just larger than needed. Discuss timing and other problems encountered in creating this procedure.

2. Write and test a DISPOSE algorithm for maintaining the LAVS by-size in ascending order of record size. Discuss the timing and difficulties encountered in designing this procedure.

3. Perform exercise two for a LAVS ordered in descending order of record size.

4. Perform exercise two for a LAVS ordered by-location address. Be very careful in creating that part of the algorithm which puts records together to form larger ones. There are three cases that must be considered, (1) the returning record gets attached to the rear of a record in the LAVS, (2) the returning record gets attached to the front of the record in the LAVS, and (3) the returning record fits between two records in the LAVS.

5. Create an example where by-size succeeds and the stack and by-location LAVS fail.

6. Create an example where the stack approach succeeds and the other two approaches fail.

7. Read the current literature and evaluate the timing of a new approach to dynamic storage management.

13

Some Interesting Problems

This chapter contains a general description of several data structure problems. Rather than filling in all the details, these problems are described as potential course projects. There are general suggestions about the appropriateness of various representations for each problem. In each case, some recommendations are made. The recommendations are only a general guide towards one approach of solving the problem. You should feel free to pursue alternate approaches.

13:1. Sparse Matrices

The solutions to many problems require matrices to represent the data. The matrix can be quite large, 50x50 or 100x100, but most of the entries are zero. Such matrices are referred to as sparse matrices. For example, one might have a 25x25 matrix with only 50 or 75 non-zero entries. Or in general, an nxn matrix can have n^2 entries but in a sparse matrix only k of these entries are non-zero for some small value of k,

$$O (k) < O (n^2).$$

Figure 13.1 is an example of a sparse matix. The problem is to find an efficient method of representing sparse matrices which is reasonably time efficient for executing most matrix arithmetic procedures. That is, the time of execution is about the same order of time as when the matrix is stored in the normal way. Also, given a sparse matrix storage method, find the maximum number of non-zero entries for which the storage method is memory efficient.

One method of storing sparse matrices in records, one record per entry, is as follows: The records are in the form

```
     1  2  3  4  5  6  7  8  9 10
  1 ⎡ 0  1  0  0  0  0  2  0  0  0 ⎤
  2 ⎢ 0  0  0  0 -3  0  0  0  0  0 ⎥
  3 ⎢ 2  0  0  3  0  0  2  0  0  0 ⎥
  4 ⎢ 0  0  7  0  0  0  0  0  3  0 ⎥
  5 ⎢ 0  0  0  0  8  0  0  0  0  0 ⎥
  6 ⎢ 0  0  0  0  0 -6  2  0  0  0 ⎥
  7 ⎢ 0  0  0  0  1  0  0  0  0  5 ⎥
  8 ⎢ 0  9  0  0  0  0  0  3  0  0 ⎥
  9 ⎢ 4  0 -3  0  0  0  0  0  0  0 ⎥
 10 ⎣ 0 -6  0  0  0  0  0  8  0  2 ⎦
```

Figure 13.1.   A Sparse Matrix


```
entryrecord =
    RECORD  rowlink: ↑entryrecord;
             collink: ↑entryrecord;
                row: integer;
             column: integer;
              entry: real
    END
```

where **rowlink** and **collink** are pointers that link together the records for their respective rows and columns. The integer entries **row** and **column** indicate the row and column for each particular entry. Then **entry** is the actual value in that position of the matrix.

These records are linked together by three other records, matrixhead, rowheader, and colheader defined as

```
matrixhead =
    RECORD rowheadlink: ↑rowheader;
            colheadlink: ↑colheader;
    END;
```

```
rowheader =
    RECORD rowlink: ↑rowheader;
            rowhead: ↑entryrecord;
             rownum: integer
    END;
```

```
colheader =
    RECORD collink: ↑colheader;
            colhead: ↑entryrecord;
             colnum: integer
    END
```

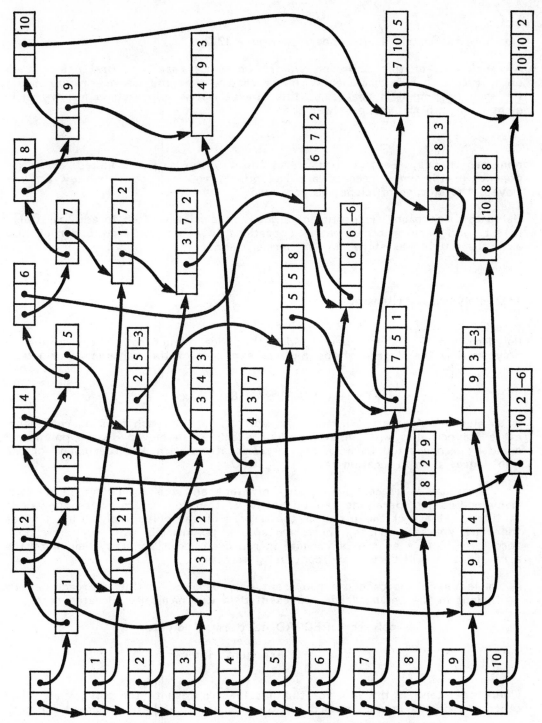

Figure 13.2. A sparse matrix, linked representation

and form the matrix as it appears in figure 13.2.

An evaluation of this approach yields two quick results. First, since each entry record has 5 components, if we assume that the memory requirements for each component is the same, this sparse matrix approach is memory efficient if an nxn matrix has fewer than

$$n^2/5$$

non-zero entries. Second, because of the way the matrix is linked, two components in the entry records are redundant, row and col. If they are removed, the storage efficiency is improved.

Using this approach, time efficient algorithms can be written to add, multiply, invert, and perform other matrix operations in about the same order of time as if the matrix was stored in the normal manner.

13:2. Polynomial Arithmetic

Polynomials are another widely used mathematical structure. The **degree of a polynomial** is the degree of the highest exponent of the variable. For example,

$$y = 24 \ x^{11} - 31 \ x^8 + 8 \ x^5 + x^2 - 4$$

is an eleventh degree polynomial. A typical first approach towards representing a polynomial is with an array. For example, an eleven degree polynomial could be represented in an array of 12 locations with the coefficient of the i-th degree term in location i+1.

This approach is reasonably memory efficient and the algorithms to perform many polynomial operations can be easily written to perform these operations in times that are of the order of the degree of the polynomial. But, just as there are sparse matrices, there are sparse polynomials with very few non-zero terms. If a sparse polynomial is represented in an array, much of the array space would be wasted, containing zero.

A simple linked approach can represent polynomials. In this approach, every coefficient in the polynomial is represented in a dynamically allocated record,

```
polyrec = RECORD nextterm: ↑polyrec·
                 coef: real;
                 exponent: integer
          END;
```

where next term is the link for the list that represents the polynomial. The other components in each record are the coefficient and the exponent for each non-zero term in the polynomial. Figure 13.3 illustrates a list that would correspond to the polynomial mentioned above.

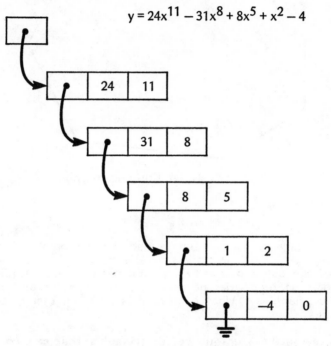

$$y = 24x^{11} - 31x^8 + 8x^5 + x^2 - 4$$

Figure 13.3. A Polynomial as a List

Using the record approach, and assuming the memory size for each type of data is the same, representing a polynomial in a dynamically allocated list is memory efficient if the number of non-zero terms is less than

$$(n+1)/3 \ .$$

With this approach, polynomials of arbitrarily large degree and few non-zero exponents can be manipulated in a time and space efficient manner. It is interesting not just to write the routines to perform polynomial arithmetic, find roots, etc., but it is also interesting to write good user interface routines that make it easy for others to input and print polynomials in a convenient manner.

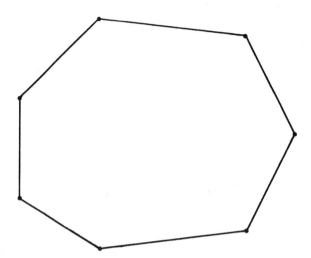

Figure 13.4. A Convex Polygon

13:3. Area of a Polygon

A polygon, see figure 13.4, can be defined by the points that are the vertices of the polygon. In general, given any polygon, create an algorithm to
find the area of the polygon. A typical approach towards finding the area of
a general polygon is to divide the polygon into triangles and find the sum of
the areas of the triangles. What is needed is an algorithm to break the polygon into triangles.

There is not necessarily a unique set of triangles that can cover the area of
a polygon. As long as one possible set of triangles is obtained, the problem
is solved. One approach towards dividing a polygon into triangles is the following: Choose a point, see figure 13.4, use this point as one of the vertices, draw all the triangles whose other two vertices are two adjacent pairs
of vertices of the polygon. This collection of triangles fills the polygon and
can be generated in a straightforward manner.

This approach fails if the polygon is concave, because some of the triangles
that would be drawn would not be completely contained in the polygon, see
figure 13.5. However, by using a queue or a stack, one can process those
triangles that are in the polygon and save the information about those vertices that form triangles that are not in the polygon.

One way to implement this is with the following algorithm: Starting with an
empty stack, begin with one node as the key node and process the polygon
as if it is convex. When a node is about to be processed that would produce a triangle that is outside of the polygon, push the key node into the

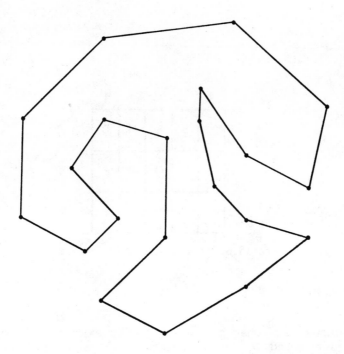

Figure 13.5.   A Non-convex Polygon

stack and use the last node that was processed as the key node. When a node has been processed and if the stack is not empty, if the node being processed, the key node, and the node at the top of the stack for a triangle that is entirely in the polygon, then process that triangle and pop the stack to obtain a new key node.

It is a good exercise to verify that this algorithm does indeed sum the areas of a set of triangles that fills the polygon. The polygon in figure 13.5 is sufficiently complex to present the possible difficulties encountered with this algorithm.

There is a simpler approach towards finding the area by summing the areas of trapezoids, as in calculus. Form trapezoids with a side containing two adjacent vertices, the x axis, and two lines from the vertices and perpendicular to the x axis. The areas of these trapezoids are considered to be signed depending upon whether the area is above or below the x axis and if the x coordinate of the second vertex is to the left or right of the first vertex, just like signed areas are formed for integration.

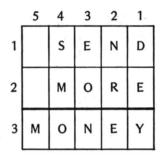

Figure 13.6.   A cryptorhythm as a matrix

13:4. Cryptorythms

A **cryptorhythm** or **alphametric** is an arithmetic expression in which the digits have all been replaced by unique letters of the alphabet.   Figure 13.6 contains an example of a cryptorhythm.   At first, one might be tempted to write a program to exhaustively search for a solution to this problem.   However, even on the fastest computer systems this would take large amounts of computer time.   Another alternative is to write an algorithm that searches for a solution of this problem in some reasonably efficient, but exhaustive manner. For example, a program might begin with the lowest ordered position, the right most column.   That is, try values for D and E, which in turn fixes a value for Y.   Then continue with the next highest order position.   Into this program one can insert tests to limit this search even further.   For example, one can quickly determine that M must equal 1.   Therefore, no other letter can take on the value one.

The next step is not so obvious, namely, write a program which reads in a cryptorhythm, then sets itself up with appropriate data structures, then solves the problem in a reasonably efficient manner.   One method of doing this is as follows: Assume the input is in the form

"base" "string"

where the base is the arithmetic base of the algorithm and string is the problem, for example,

10 SEND+MORE=MONEY.

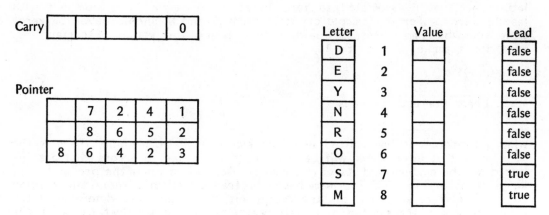

Figure 13.7. Data structures for solving cryptorhythms

From this, the program can scan and determine the size of the cryptorhythm and, therefore, the sizes of the necessary structures. If the problem is thought of as being represented by a two dimensional array as in figure 13.6, then the algorithm would set up the structures as shown in figure 13.7. The program could use a two dimensional array of pointers to correspond the one occurrence of the value of each letter to the possibly many occurrences of that letter in the cryptorhythm. In addition, a two dimensional array of logical values indicates the first location, with respect to the order of processing, of each letter in the puzzle. The reason for the logical array becomes apparent in the algorithm for solving cryptorhythms as described below.

With the arrays structured as indicated, the algorithm finds the solutions for each puzzle by processing each column of the two dimensional array of pointers starting with the right most column. By looking at the corresponding position in the two dimensional array of logical values, the algorithm can determine if the values for the letter can be exhaustively attempted. If it can, it selects the next possible value for the letter. If one exists, the program continues, if not, it resets the value that corresponds to that letter and backtracks to the previous letter that can be reset. If it succeeds in setting values for each letter in the column, it then tests to see if the arithmetic for that column is satisfied. In checking the arithmetic for a column, the program uses the carryover from the previous column and sets the carry into the next column. If the arithmetic is satisfied for a column, the program continues by processing the next column. If not, the program must backtrack and reset the value or values corresponding to letters.

There are many enhancements that can be made to this approach. For example, to improve the timing of the program, a test can be made so that leading letters are never associated to zero because we never write numbers with leading zeros. For the sample cryptorhythm, S and M should never be zero. Other possible improvements would include fixing the values of certain letters, for example, M must be 1.

13:5. Error Correcting Codes

When information is transmitted using an electromagnetic medium, there is the possibility that information will be lost or changed due to errors that are induced by the medium and its environment. Depending upon the probability of an error occurring, the information can be transmitted in a redundant fashion so that the receiver can check the redundant information and determine if the information was transmitted successfully. One of the simplest cases of the transmission of redundant information is the normal storage of information on magnetic tapes. Typically, the information is stored on magnetic tapes with **parity**. That is, on a 9 track tape drive, eight tracks are used to store information and the ninth track stores a parity check. If the tapes are stored with odd parity, then the ninth track is set to 0 or 1 so that the number of one bits across the tape is odd. In this way the tape reading mechanism can quickly check to see if an error occurs. This is under the assumption that there is a very high probability that at most one bit might be incorrectly recorded (which is a reasonable assumption). With even parity, the count of the number of one bits across the tape is even. Figure 13.8 illustrates the storage of bits on a 9 track tape using odd parity.

Unfortunately, this approach only checks for errors, it does not locate the exact position of the error. This is sometimes referred to as an **error checking code**. In the case of a tape drive, it is usually a simple problem to re-read the data. Often, by just rereading the data, the information can be read correctly. But suppose the information is being transmitted from a satellite and because of the distance and time involved, it is impossible to reread the information. Also, in the case of a satellite, there is an even higher degree of probability of errors occurring in transmission because of interference from a variety of sources.

What is desirable in the case of satellite transmission and other cases where it is very inconvenient to have the data retransmitted is an **error correcting code**. An error correcting code is a code which contains enough redundant information so that if some small amount of data is changed, there is still enough information to correct the error without having the data retransmitted.

The assumption of this example is that seven bits of information are transmitted with the very high probability (almost 1.00) that at most one bit of in-

	1	1	1	1	0	0	
	1	0	1	0	0	1	
	0	0	1	0	0	0	
	1	0	1	0	0	1	
	0	1	0	1	0	0	
	0	0	0	0	0	1	
	1	1	1	0	0	0	
	0	0	1	0	0	1	
Parity	1	0	1	1	1	1	

Information brackets the first eight rows.

Figure 13.8. Odd Parity 9-Track Tape Format

formation is changed. This approach can be easily generalized to other cases where

$$2^n - 1$$

bits can be transmitted with probability 1 that at most 1 bit is changed.

To understand how this works, consider the Venn Diagram in figure 13.9. Assume that 4 bits of information are transmitted along with 3 bits of redundant information for error correcting. Each of the four bits of information corresponds to one of four areas in the Venn diagram that correspond to the intersection of two or more of the three sets A, B, and C. As a result, a bit is corresponded to 3 of the four areas that make up each of these sets. The fourth area in each set now has a 0 or 1 corresponded to it so that the number of 1s in each set is odd. The result is an odd parity check in each set. Now, if any one of the seven bits is changed, a parity check in each set can determine if any bit in that set was changed. Then, the collected information about the three sets determines which bit, if any, must be corrected. For example, assume that bit r was changed. Then the parity checks in sets A and B would fail and the parity check for set C would succeed. Therefore the error is in the subset given by the expression

$$A \mathrel{\&} B \mathrel{\&} (\neg C) = \{r\}.$$

A simple way of carrying out this set oriented error correcting process is to associate each set to a power of 2 (1,2,4), say

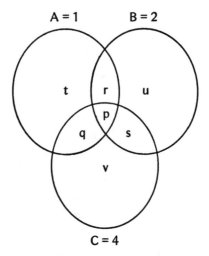

Figure 13.9. A Venn Diagram

$$1 - A$$
$$2 - B$$
$$4 - C$$

Then the position of each bit in a seven bit pattern is determined by the sum of the numbers that correspond to the sets that it is in, namely,

subset	no.	bits CBA	subset	no.	bits CBA
t	1	001	q	5	101
u	2	010	s	6	110
r	3	011	p	7	111
v	4	100			

Then determine which bits are in a particular set, say B, by simply looking at the binary representation of the bit's position in the bit pattern. If the set's bit is on, B's bit is 2, then that bit position contains a bit from that set (u, r, s, and p are in B).

The transition from Venn Diagrams arithmetic allows this approach to use more sets. For example, if 15 bits could be transmitted with probability 1 that at most only one bit will be changed, then with this approach four sets allow eleven bits of information to be transmitted with only four bits for error correcting. If 31 bits could be transmitted, then 5 error correcting bits would be transmitted with 26 bits of information using 5 sets.

SETS	INFO. BITS	CORR.BITS	EFFECIENCY
3	4	3	.57
4	11	4	.73
5	26	5	.84
n	2^n-n-1	n	$(2^n-n-1)/(2^n-1)$

Figure 13.10.   Table of Error Correcting Code Transmission Efficiency

The table in figure 13.10 illustrates the possible transmission efficiency for information given the number of bits that can be transmitted together using this approach. Writing a program to carry out, using bit manipulation, this error correcting approach, both for transmission and reception, is a good exercise. It demonstrates the close relationships between set algebra, logic, and the basic binary representations of numbers.

13:6. EXERCISES

1.   Write and test procedures to perform matrix operations on sparse matrices kept as linked structures. Also, write some user interface procedures to create and print sparse matrices. Procedures should be written to add, subtract, multiply, and invert sparse matrices.

2.   Write and test procedures to manipulate polynomials that are kept as linked lists. Include procedures to set up and print polynomials. Procedures should be written to add, subtract, multiply, and divide polynomials. Also, procedures to find the roots, or at least the real roots, of polynomials would be useful (see problem 4 below). Two useful procedures would be a rule-of-signs procedure to determine the maximum number of positive and negative roots and a synthetic division procedure to help search for roots.

3.   Write and test error correcting code routines that are generalized so that they can work for several sizes (7, 15, 31).

4.   Write and test a routine to find roots of a polynomial stored as a list.

5.   Write and test a routine that finds the area of a polygon.

14

Data Structures
and Data Base Systems

Data Base Systems are systems for collecting, storing, and retrieving large collections of information in a non-redundant manner so that the relationships between items can be maintained and programs can extract information from the collection in some reasonably efficient manner. A primary concern is overall efficiency at the possible cost of some efficiency for some programs accessing the data base of information. Included in the concerns of those responsible for the maintenance of data base systems is the integrity of the data. That is, that the base of information contains no error, accidental or deliberate. Another concern is for privacy. That is, that only those who are allowed access to certain information can actually access it.

Because of the large amount of information, the data cannot be stored in the main memory of a computing system. Instead, it is normally stored on other devices, like disks, etc., which have timing characteristics different from the timing characteristics of main memory. For disks there are at least two major differences. First, while main memory times are measured in nanoseconds or microseconds, disk times are measured in milliseconds, a thousand to a million times slower. Second, disks are not truely random access devices. The access time does depend upon the location of data, and it is not independent of the location or the time of the previous access. This affects the time required to position the disk's read/write mechanism and other factors.

From a data structures point of view, building a data base system is applying data structures concepts to the organization of information on pseudorandom access devices and attempting to carry this out in an efficient manner. This problem is compounded by the problems of security and integrity by the large number of diverse users who must access the data. This chapter is but a brief glimpse into data base with an emphasis only on the logical structure of data base management systems. A variety of texts are available with much more thorough presentations.

14:1. Data Base Management Systems

Historically, the term **data base** evolves from various attempts by companies to control the storage of information on computing systems. Typically, multiple copies of information were kept with as many as one copy for each program using the information. If a correction is made, each copy of the data has to be corrected or there is the distinct possibility of programs using erroneous data. This leads to a problem of verifying the accuracy of information. One reason for multiple copies of data was that one user might be interested in the data in one context while another user might be concerned about different relationships among the data. Attempts to eliminate the redundancy, guarantee accuracy, and satisfy the needs of various users of a collection of information led to the development of Data Base Management Systems (DBMS).

A complete discussion of DBMS is beyond the scope of this text. However, one aspect of DBMS is closely related to this text, namely, the problem of describing the logical relationships between data given the physical constraints of the devices that store the data. In addition, most DBMSs have limitations on the types of relationships that can be defined between data items, or when relations can be defined between data items.

There are three distinct approaches towards the logical organization of information in a DBMS. These are referred to as the **hierarchical**, the **network**, and the **relational** approaches. An overview of each appears in subsequent sections. But before these three approaches are presented, a set of basic terminology is needed.

The fundamental term in data base is **entity**. An entity is an object or event that is represented by some collection of data. An occurrence of an entity is a collection of data that describes each of the elementary items in the entity.

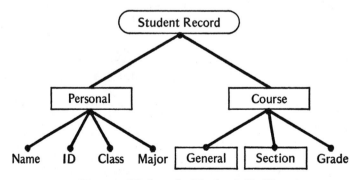

Figure 14.1. A Student Entity

For example, an entity could be a student's semester course schedule, STUDENT RECORD. The entity, see figure 14.1, could include the name of the student, his student identification number, class, major, and information about each course that he is taking. For each course the student takes, there is a course department, course number, section number, the course name, instructor, room, and time assignments. The student's name, ID, class and major are referred to as **elementary items.** The course information however is really a collection of from zero to many entries. Such an item is often referred to as a **repeating group.** Actually, in this case, the "course" is also an entity and many relationships exist between entities and various occurrences of entities. In this case, the COURSE entity is a **member** of the STUDENT RECORD entity, or the STUDENT RECORD entity **owns** the COURSE entity. An **occurrence** of an entity is a collection of information that satisfies all components of the entity.

If one is concerned with some of the lower level details of representing the connection between an arbitrary number of courses in each student record, think of it as a list, possibly empty, of pointers that point to the appropriate collection of information.

Depending upon the information that one wishes to obtain, there are many possible combinations of results. Between a student and his ID, a **one-to-one** relation exists. For a student, a **one-to-many** relationship exists between a student and the courses that he is taking. For a department within a school, a **many-to-many** relationship exists between its courses and the students taking these courses. The ability to conveniently form one-to-one, one-to-many, and many-to-many relationships is an important aspect of a data base model.

Given the base of data, the variety of information that one wishes to obtain from this data base, and the physical devices storing the data, how should the information be organized so that all potential users of the data can conveniently access it? What is desired is a simple and generalizable method for structuring the data so that as new data and new relationships between the data evolve, the base of information and its structure remain adaptable to new program requests without destroying the access to the data by existing programs.

There are three clearly recognizable data models:

1. Hierarchical;
2. Network or Graphical;
3. Relational.

The following sections contain brief overviews of each of these models. To illustrate the similarities, differences, advantages, and disadvantages of each data model, the structure illustrated in figure 14.1 illustrates a relationship between various items of information that form a foundation for many questions that could be answered from the information derived from the relations. It is fair to assume that in storing a data model, the elementary data items and their logical connections are stored on some mass storage device and that

```
01  STUDENT RECORD
    02  PERSONAL
        03  NAME
        03  ID
        03  CLASS
        03  MAJOR
    02  COURSE occurs 0 to n times
        03  GENERAL
            04  DEPARTMENT
            04  NUMBER
            04  TITLE
        03  SECTION
            04  NUMBER
            04  TIME
            04  INSTRUCTOR
        03  GRADE
```

Figure 14.2. A COBOL-like description of 14.1

some method, for example, pointers, is used to link data together logically. Given this structured base of information, a variety of questions can be asked and information can be obtained, for example:

1. Generate a course schedule for each student;
2. Generate a class list for each class;
3. Generate a list of classes for each teacher;
4. Generate a list of sections for each course.

From a data structures stand point, a goal of data base is to store the information so that these and all other reasonable questions that one might ask about the data can be answered in some reasonably efficient amount of time.

14:2. The Hierarchical Data Model

The hierarchical data model can be best understood through its evolution. It evolved from the COBOL record concept. A COBOL-like model of the entity in figure 14.1 appears in figure 14.2. The level numbers indicate a further break down or clarification of the information at the preceding level. The structure between records is tree-like containment. Each item in a record is contained in the first item above it with the next lowest level number. Also, some items, contain others because they were subdivided. There is no ambiguity in the fact that NUMBER appears twice in the description. In each case, NUMBER is a member of a different higher level item. That is, there is no problem distinguishing between a course NUMBER and a section NUMBER of a course. To avoid ambiguity, the two NUMBERs are referred to as

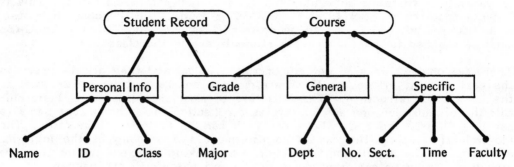

Figure 14.3.   STUDENT entity with shared components

COURSE NUMBER and SECTION NUMBER when there is a possibility of confusion.

Logically, the COBOL-like containment structure is equivalent to the hierarchical data model. This model has some constraints imposed on it simply because of the order forced onto data by the tree structure of the model. In particular, the root of the tree, see figure 14.3, **owns** the rest of the tree, and every member in the tree owns the items under it. Therefore, if STUDENT RECORD and COURSE are considered entities, the STUDENT RECORD owns COURSE because of the hierarchical structure of the information.

First, member entities cannot be shared. That is, the semester records of two students could not share the course information although they are in the same section of the course. Second, no member can contain a higher level entry. That is, suppose someone, the instructor, wishes to have a class list for his course. This would be equivalent to wanting another hierarchical structure with class at the top and student as a repeating group under it. Both of these problems can be handled by carefully choosing the hierarchical structures, distinguishing between relations, and loosening the constraints of membership to allow for shared ownership.

The first restriction, sharing entities, can be relaxed to improve storage efficiency. This could be viewed as a restructuring of the STUDENT RECORD entity so that the repeating group COURSE has two components, the student's grade in the course and the course information, that could be shared between occurrences of the STUDENT RECORD entity. This shared component could simply be carried out with a pointer from a STUDENT RECORD occurrence to the occurrence of the appropriate COURSE entities. This is illustrated in figure 14.4.

In the hierarchical data model, inquiries whose question/answer relationships follow the hierarchy lend themselves to answering in reasonable amounts of

time. That is, since COURSE is a member of STUDENT RECORD, it is easier
to generate a student's schedule than it is to generate a class list. This is
because once the right STUDENT RECORD is found, the schedule information
is in that record. However, to generate a class list, all STUDENT RECORDs
must be scanned to determine which students are in the class.

There are obvious ways to get out of this problem and they are discussed in
the next section. However, there are many problems that lend themselves to
the hierarchical structure. The structure of most organizations is hierarchical, the organization of many objects as a collection of its component parts (a
car is a chassis and body, both of which can be further subdivided). The
hierarchical model is the easiest to implement and as long as the inquiries
made against the model can be answered by making efficient use of the tree
structure, programs can function in a time and space efficient manner.

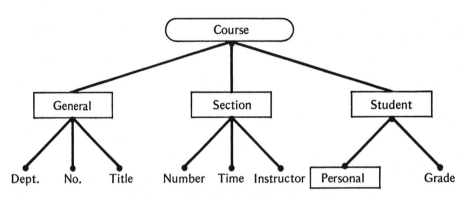

Figure 14.4.   COURSE Entity Owner Hierarchy

14:3. The Graphical Model

As one works more and more with the hierarchical model, eventually the need
for entity A to own entity B which in turn owns entity A leads to the graphical or network model. For example, besides the hierarchies in figures 14.3
and figure 14.4, it would also be nice to have the hierarchy in figure 14.5
because the tree structure in figure 14.5 lends itself to creating class lists.
But the multiple hierarchies create problems unless they are kept under some
control. It is desirable to maintain some limitations, in particular:

   1.   An entity is not allowed to be both a member in and a member of the
        same entity;

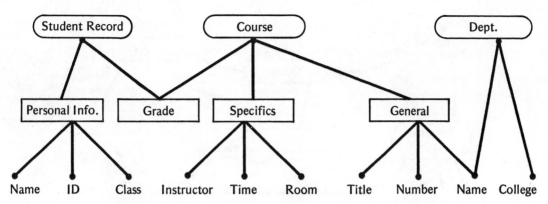

Figure 14.5.   A Free Tree of Multiple Hierarchies

2.   The sharing by entities of members is restricted so that the graph of the result is a free tree.

One way of thinking of this for our sample problem appears in figure 14.6. Here, our data model is composed of a multiple hierarchical data model which links hierarchies together by sharing common members.   The result is a free tree, that is, there is one and only one path from any one point in any hierarchy to another point in any hierarchy.   This result is still normally considered a hierarchical structure in most of the data base literature, but when considered from a data structures point of view, the additional pointers that are needed so that one can conveniently traverse paths through these various hierarchical structures, it is easy to see that this is a substantially more complex model to work with.   Once the restrictions are removed, in particular, the "free tree" restriction, the data model becomes a **graphical** , or **network** model.

In the network model, since there can be multiple paths between items, it is important to label the arcs between items in order to distinguish between the paths and the relationships between nodes in the network.   Figure 14.6 illustrates a network data model of our student information base.   In this model, since multiple paths can occur (a student can be both a major in some department and take courses in the same department) the relations between entities are labelled.   This model is more general in that it does not have a bias towards any particular entity.   However, this does present a trade-off when viewed relative to a hierarchical data model.   In the hierarchical data model, the structures that were followed to answer certain questions could be easily defined, while others required a more exhaustive search process.   In the network model of figure 14.6, because of the greater variety of links between entities, one simply starts at the appropriate entity and describes the links to be used to answer the inquiry.

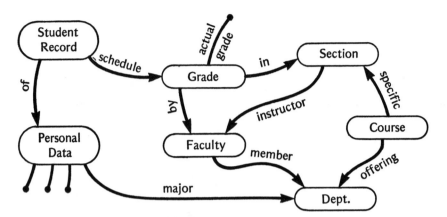

Figure 14.6.   A Network Data Model

To illustrate, consider the two inquiries:

1. List all grades that students received in Computer Science courses;
2. List all Computer Science Majors.

In both cases, the inquiry is answered by starting with the DEPT entity and finding the occurrence of Computer Science. The first inquiry is answered by following the "offering" link to COURSE entities, the "section of" link, the reverse link of "in" to get to GRADEs, then finally, the link between GRADE and STUDENT to get a list of all students by grade in each section of each computer science course. The second question can be answered by simply following the "majors" link to the list of students majoring in Computer Science courses.

In summary, one can see that the trade-off between the hierarchical and the network models is between a more complex linking between entities, which requires more storage, versus a broader collection of inquiries that can be handled with reasonable efficiency.

14:4. The Relational Model

After looking at the other two data models, the relational model appears foreign in its approach. This model is based on set theory and the use of set concepts to obtain information. The first obvious observation is that the concept of containment of entities does not exist. There are only relationships between entities. In the relational model, entities are defined by n-tuples. Figure 14.7 illustrates several n-tuples describing some of the entities that were discussed in the previous sections. Assuming that the relation concept can be efficiently stored and accessed, logic, predicate calculus and relational algebra, like concepts describe inquiries against the relational data model.

STUDENT_PERSONAL = [ID_NUM, NAME, CLASS, MAJOR]

STUDENT_ENTRY = [ID_NUM, DEPT, COURSE_NUM, SECTION, GRADE]

COURSE = [DEPT, SECTION, ROOM, TIME, INSTRUCTOR]

Figure 14.7. Example Relational Data Model N-Tuples

For example, to create class list, the inquiry against the data model would ask

list all STUDENT_PERSONAL.NAME where for STUDENT_ENTRY
[(STUDENT_PERSONAL.ID_NUM = STUDENT_ENTRY.ID_NUM) &
(STUDENT_ENTRY.DEPT = "CMPS") &
(STUDENT_ENTRY.COURSE_NUM = "110") &
(STUDENT_ENTRY.SECTION = "2")].

This lists the names of all students whose ID_NUM matches the ID_NUM in STUDENT_ENTRY if the department, course number, and section is CMPS 110, section 2. Similarly, a student's schedule is defined as

list all (COURSE.DEPT, COURSE.COURSE_NUM, COURSE.SECTION,
COURSE.TIME) when
(STUDENT_ENTRY.ID = "student id") &
(STUDENT_ENTRY.COURSE_NUM = COURSE.COURSE_NUM)

This would result in a complete listing of all the information a student might need for his schedule.

Logically, one can envision n-tuples in the relational data model as tables that list the collections of data that satisfy the relation. At the physical level, there are a variety of ways to carry this out. Figure 14.8 illustrates a part of the table for the STUDENT_ENTRY relation. This table might be implemented as a linked list of pointers to the locations of the actual data items that form each relation, see figure 14.9. In reality, the actual representation in a particular system might be more complicated because of the specifics of the particular device that stores the information as well as the structures that represent the relational data models.

STUDENT_ENTRY

ID_NUM	DEPT	COURSE	SECTION	GRADE
111223333	CMPS	110	2	B
111223333	ENGL	3	8	C
111223333	CMPS	125	1	A
987654321	HIST	31	12	C
987654321	ENGL	3	4	B
555443321	ENGL	3	8	A
555443321	CMPS	125	1	C
111223333	HIST	1	15	B
987654321	MATH	12	3	A
555443321	MATH	12	3	B

Figure 14.8. A Table Representation of a Relational Model

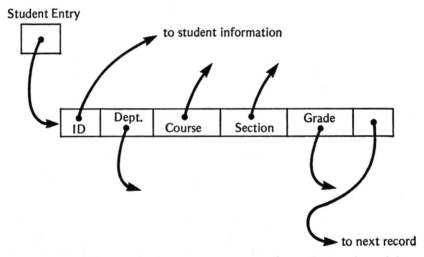

Figure 14.9. Linked representation of a relational model

14:5. Observations

A data base model must be able to represent a variety of relationships in an efficient manner. The basic hierarchical model can represent one-to-one and one-to-many relations, but cannot efficiently represent many-to-many relations. The apparent limitations of the hierarchical model are relaxed by a model which allows hierarchies to share items. With this model, much can be accomplished. Also, although it might not be computer efficient in answering some requests, the hierarchical model tends to be human efficient. That is, it is relatively easy for one human to describe to another human how an inquiry is answered through the data model. Carrying out that inquiry is another matter.

The network or graphical model is a natural generalization of the hierarchical model. The data base management system described in the report of the CODASYL Data Base Task Group in 1971 is based on this type of model. Many references to this can be found in data base literature. Included in the literature on the hierarchical data model is a Data Description Language (DDL) and a variety of methods of graphically representing this data model.

The relational model takes a completely different approach which makes heavy use of set theory and logic. However, in all three cases, when viewing implementations of this and other models, there are concerns for the variety of updates of the data base that must occur. In particular, when new items are included and old items are deleted, how does the data base system efficiently handle the variety of linking and relinking problems it encounters?

14:6. EXERCISES

1. Create a hierarchy chart of the corporate structure of your college or university. Determine several inquiries that can be efficiently handled using that structure. Determine several inquiries that could not be efficiently handled. 2. For your county, create the hierarchical structure that represents the various taxing municipalities in the county (township, borough, city, town, etc.).

3. Draw a network data model to illustrate the relationship between various administrative components on your college or university (treasurer, registrar, dean, computer center, etc.).

4. Create a new network data model so that the following questions could be conveniently answered:

   a. Create lists of all freshman, sophomores, etc.;
   b. Create lists of students by major.

5. The classification of plants in Biology forms a hierarchical structure. Create programs to create, update, and make inquiries about biological objects using a hierarchical data model.

Bibliography

1. AUSTING, R. H., and G. L. ENGEL, **A Computer Science Program for Small Colleges,** Comm. ACM 16(3): 139-148, March 1973.

2. AUSTING, R. H., et. al., **Curriculum '78: Recommendations for the Undergraduate Program in Computer Science** - A Report of the ACM Curriculum Committee on Computer Science, Comm. ACM 22(3): 147-165, March 1979.

3. BAER,J.L. and B.SCHWAB, **A Comparison of Tree-Balancing Algorithms,** Comm. ACM 20(5), May,1977.

4. BAYER,R. and C.Mccreight, **Organization and Maintainance of Large Ordered Indexes,** Acta Informatica, 1(3): 173-89,1972.

5. BAYER,R. and J.METZGER, **On Encipherment of Search Trees and Random Access Files,** ACM Trans. Database Syst., 1(1): 37-52, March 1976.

6. BAYER,R., **Binary B-trees for Virtual Memory,** Proc. 1971 ACM SIGFIDET Workshop: 219-25. ACM,New York.

7. BAYER,R., **Symmetric Binary B-Trees: Data Structures and Maintainance Algorithms,** Acta Informatica, 1(4): 290-306, 1972.

8. BERGE,C., **Theory of Graphs and its Applications,** Methuen Press, 1962.

9. BERZTISS,A.T., **Data Structures, Theory and Practice,** 2d ed., Academic Press, New York, 1977.

10. BITNER,J.R. and E.M.REINGOLD, **Backtrack Programming Techniques,** Comm. ACM., 18: 651-56, 1975.

11. BLUM,M., R.W.FLOYD, V.PRAT, R.L.RIVEST, and R.E.TARJAN, **Time Bounds for Selection,** J. Comput. Sys. Sci., 7: 448-61, 1973.

12. BOOTHROYD,J, **Algorithm 201(Shellsort),** Comm. ACM, 6: 445, 1963.

13. BROWN,M., **A Storage Scheme for Height-Balanced Trees,** Inf. Proc. Lett., 7(5): 231-32, August 1978.

14. BROWN,M.R., **A Storage Scheme for Height-Balanced Trees,** Info. Proc. Letters 7,5: 231-232, August 1978.

15. BUCHHOLZ,W., **File organization and addressing,** IBM Syst. J. 2: 86-111, June 1963.

16. BURGE,W.H., **A Correspondence Between Two Sorting Methods,** IBM Research Report RC 6395, Thomas J. Watson Research Center, Yorktown Heights, N.Y., 1977

17. BURGE,W.H., **Sorting, trees, and measures of order,** Inform. and Control 1(3): 181-197, 1968.

18. CARTER,J.L. and M.N.WEGMAN, **Universal Classes of Hash Functions,** IBM Research Report RC 6495, Thomas J. Watson Research Center, Yorktown Heights, N.Y., 1977

19. CICHELLI,R.J., **Minimal Perfect Hash Functions Made Simple,** Comm. ACM, 23(1), January 1980.

20. CLAMPETT,H, **Randomized Binary Searching With Tree Structures,** Comm. ACM, 7(3): 163-65, Mar. 1964.

21. COMER,D., **The Ubiquitous B-Tree,** ACM Computing Surveys, 11(2), June 1979.

22. COUGAR, J. D.(ed), **Curriculum Recommendations for Undergraduate Programs in Information Systems,** CACM 16,12: 727-749, December 1973.

23. Curriculum Committee on Computer Science, **Curriculum '68: Recommendations for Academic Programs in Computer Science** Comm. ACM 11(3): 151-197, March 1968.

24. DENNING,P., **Virtual Memory,** Comp. Surveys, 2(3): 153-189, 1970.

25. DRISCOLI,J.R. and Y.E.LIEN, **A Selective Traversal Algorithm for Binary Search Trees,** Comm. ACM, 21(6), June 1978.

26. ELSON,M., **Data Structures,** Science Reasearch Associates, Palo Alto, Ca., 1975.

27. FLORES,I., **Computer Sorting,** Prentice-Hall, Englewood Cliffs, N.J., 1969.

28. FLOYD,R.W. and R.L.RIVEST, **Algorithm 489(Select),** Comm. ACM, 18(3): 173, March 1975.

29. FLOYD,R.W. and R.L.RIVEST, **Expected Time Bounds for Selection,** Comm. ACM, 18(3), March 1975.

30. FLOYD,R.W., **Algorithm 245(Treesort3),** Comm. ACM., 7: 701, 1964.

31. FOSTER,C.C., **A Generalization of AVL Trees,** Comm. ACM, 16(8), August 1973.

32. FRANTA,W.R. and K.MALY, **A Comparison of Heaps and the TL Structure for the Simulation Event Set** Comm. ACM, 21(10), October 1978.

33. FRAZER,W.D. and A.C.McKELLAR, **Samplesort: A Sampling Approach to Minimal Storage Tree Sorting,** J. ACM, 17(3), July 1970.

34. GARSIA,A.M. and M.L.WACHS, **A New Algorithm for Minimum Cost Binary Trees,** SIAM J. Comp., 6(4), December 1977.

35. GHOSH,S.P. and V.Y.LUM, **Analysis of Collisions when Hashing by Division,** Inf. Syst., 1: 15-22, 1975.

36. GONNET,G.H. and MUNRO,I., **The Analysis of an Improved Hashing Technique,** Proc. 9th Ann. ACM Symposium on the Theory of Computing, 113-121, May, 1977.

37. GOTLIEB,C.C. and TOMPA,F.W., **Choosing a Storage Schema,** Acta Informatica 3, 297-320, 1974.

38. GOTLIEB,C.C., **Sorting on Computers,** Comm ACM 6(5), pp.194-201.

39. GROGONO,P., **Programming in Pascal,** Addison-Wesley, Reading, Mass., 1978.

40. HARARY,F., **Graph Theory,** Addison-Wesley, Boston, 1969.

41. HELD,G. and M.STONEBRAKER, **B-trees Re-examined,** Comm. ACM, 21(2): 139-43, Febuary 1978.

42. HIBBARD,T.N., **Some combinational properties of certain trees with applications to searching and sorting,** J. ACM 9(1): pp.13-28, January 1962.

43. HIRSCHBERG,D.S., **A class of dynamic memory allocation algorithms,** Comm ACM 16(10): 615-618, October, 1973.

44. HOARE,C., **Notes on Data Structuring,** "Structured Programming"(DAHL,DIJKSTRA, HOARE), Academic Press, New York, 1972.

45. HOARE,C.A.R and N. WIRTH, **An Axiomatic Definition of the Programming Language Pascal,** Acta Informatica, 2(4), 1973.

46. HOPCROFT,J. and J.ULLMAN, **Formal Languages and their Relations to Automata,** Addison-Wesley, Boston 1969.

47. HOROWITZ,E. and S.SAHNI, **Algorithms: Design and Analysis,** Computer Science Press, Potomac, Md., 1977.

48. HOROWITZ,E. and S.SAHNI, **Fundamentals of Data Structures,** Computer Science Press, Woodland Hills, Calif., 1975.

49. KERNIGHAN,B. and P.J.PLAUGER, **Software Tools,** Addison-Wesley, Reading, Mass., 1976.

50. KIEBURTZ,R.B., **Structured Programming and Problem-Solving with Pascal,** Prentice-Hall, Englewood Cliffs,N.J. 1978.

51. KNUTH,D.E., **Fundamental Algorithms,** 2d ed., Addison-Wesley, Reading, Mass., 1973.

52. KNUTH,D.E., **Optimum Binary Search Trees,** Acta Informatica, 1: 14-25, 1971.

53. KNUTH,D.E., **Sorting and Searching,** Addison-Wesley, Reading, Mass., 1973.

54. KNUTH,D.E., **Structured Programming with Goto Statements,** ACM Computing Surveys, 6(4): 261, December 1974.

55. KORFHAGE,R.R., **Discrete Computational Structures,** Academic Press, New York, 1974.

56. LESK,M.E., **Compressed Text Storage,** Bell Labs. Tech. Rept. 3: 34, November 1970.

57. LEWIS,T.G. and M.Z.SMITH, **Applying Data Structures,** Houghton Mifflin, Boston, 1976.

58. LOESER,R., **Some Performance Tests of 'Quicksort' and Descendants,** Comm. ACM, 17(3), March 1974.

59. LUCCIO,F. and L.PAGLI, **On the Height of Height-Balanced Trees,** IEEE Trans. Comptrs., (1), January 1976.

60. McCREIGHT,E.M., **Pagination of B*-Trees with Variable Length Records,** Comm. ACM 20(9): 670-674, Septemebr 1977.

61. MARTIN,J., **Principles of Data-Base Management,** Prentice-Hall, Englewood Cliffs, New Jersey, 1976.

62. MARTIN,W., **Sorting,** Comp. Surveys, 3(4): 147, 1971.

63. MARUYAMA,K. and SMITH,S.E., **Optimal Reorganizations of Distributed Space Disk Files,** CACM 19(11): 634-642, November 1976.

64. MAURER,H.A., **Data Structures and Programming Techniques,** Prentice-Hall, Englewood Cliffs, N.J., 1977.

65. MAURER,W. and T.LEWIS, **Hash Table Methods,** Comp. Surveys, 7(1): 5-19, March 1975.

66. MORRIS,R., **Scatter Storage Techniques,** Comm. ACM, 11(1): 38-44, January 1968.

67. NEWELL,A. and SHAW,J.C., **The Logic Theory Machine,** Proc. Western JCC, 230-240, 1957

68. NIEVERGELT,J. and E.M.REINGOLD, **Binary Search Trees of Bounded Balance,** SIAM J. Comp., 2: 33, 1973.

69. NIEVERGELT,J., **Binary Search Trees and File Organization,** ACM Computing Surveys, 6(3), September 1974.

70. PERL,Y., A.ITAI, and H.AVNI, **Interpolation Search-A Log Log N Search,** Comm. ACM, 21: 550-57, 1978.

71. PFALTZ,J.L., **Computer Data Structures,** McGraw-Hill, New York, 1977.

72. POHL,I., **A Sorting Problem and its Complexity,** Comm. ACM, 15(6), June 1972.

73. POHL,I., **Bi-Directional Search,** Machine Intelligence 6, 127-140, 1971.

74. POLYA,G., **How to Solve it,** Doubleday, Garden City, N.Y., 1957.

75. PRICE,C., **Table Lookup Techniques,** ACM Comp. Surveys. 3(2): 49-65, 1971.

76. RIVEST,R.L. and KNUTH,D.E., **Bibliography 26: Computing Sorting,** Computing Reviews 13,6: 283-289, June 1972.

77. ROSE,L. and GOTTERER,M.H., **A Theory of Dynamic File Management in a Multilevel Store,** Int. J. of Comp. & Inf. Sci. 2, 249-256, 1973.

78. SCOWEN,R.S., **Algorithm 271, Quickersort,** Comm ACM 8(11): pp.669-670, Novemeber 1965.

79. SEDGEWICK,R., **Implementing Quicksort Programs,** Comm. ACM, 21(10), October 1978.

80. SEDGEWICK,R., **Permutation Generation Methods,** ACM Computing Surveys, 9(2): 137, June 1977.

81. SHELL,D.L., **A High Speed Sorting Procedure,** Comm. ACM, 2(7), July 1959.

82. SHELL,D.L., **Optimizing the polyphase sort,** Comm ACM 14(11): pp.713-719, Novemeber 1971.

83. SHNEIDERMAN,B., **Jump Searchimg: A Fast Sequential Search Technique,** Comm. ACM, 21(10), October 1978.

84. STANFEL,L.E., **Tree Structures for Optimal Searching,** JACM 17,3: 508-517, July 1970.

85. STONE,H., **Introduction to Computer Organization and Data Structures,** McGraw-Hill, New York, 1972.

86. SUNDGREN,B., **Theory of Data Bases,** Mason-Charter, London, 1975.

87. TARJAN,R.E. and A.C.YAO, **Storing a Sparse Table,** Comm. ACM, 22(11), November 1979.

88. TENENBAUM,A., **Simulations of Dynamic Sequential Search Algorithms,** Comm. ACM, 21(9), September 1978.

89. TREMBLAY,J.P. and P.G.SORENSON, **An Introduction to Data Structures with Applications,** McGraw-Hill, New York, 1976.

90. VAN EMDEN,M.H., **Increasing the efficiency of Quicksort, Algorithm 402,** Comm ACM 13(11): pp.693-694, Novemeber 1970.

91. VUILLEMIN,J., **A Unifying Look at Data Structures,** Comm. ACM, 23(4), April 1980.

92. WEGBREIT,B., **A Space-Efficient List Structure Tracing Algorithm,** IEEE Trans. Comp. 21(9): 1009-1010, September 1972.

93. WICKELGREN,W.A., **How to Solve Problems: Elements of a Theory of Problems and Problem Solving,** Freeman, San Francisco, 1974.

94. WINDLEY,P.F., **Trees, forests and rearranging,** British Comput. J. 3(2): pp.84-88, 1960.

95. WIRTH,N., **The Programming Language Pascal,** Acta Informatica, 1(1), 1971.

96. ZWEBEN,S.H. and McDONALD,M.A., **An Optimal Method for Deletions in One-Sided Height-Balanced Trees,** Comm. ACM 21(6): 441-445, June 1978·

Index

address calculation 154
allocation,dynamic 70,167
arc 42
available spave,list of 168
avl-tree 123-127
    balance 123
    four rebalancings 126
    restructuring 127
balanced tree 46
big O 23, 28
binary tree 87, 92
    dynamic 92
    in an array 88
    in records 92
bisection search 152
block sequential search 158
border crossing 43,120,121
bubble sort 134,135
bumping problem 62
child pointer 94
circular list 80
codes,error checking 186
codes,error correcting 186
cryptorhythm 183
cycle 42
data base 194
data model,graphical 208
    hierarchical 196
    network 208
    relational 212
data structures 1
dictionary tree 48,98
digraph 43,107
    path in 43
    triangular matrix of a 110
directed graph(see digraph)
dispose procedure 169
dominance 23
double ended queue 82, 41
dynamic allocation 70

entity(data base) 194
error correcting codes 186
exchange sort 134
exponential timing 34
fibonacci sequence 146
fifo 40, 51
four color problem 43,118,122
free tree 44
garbage collection 172
graph 42,107
    algorithm speed-up 117
    arc incidence table 113
    connected 43
    connection table 112
    linked representation 114
    matrix of a 107
    vector representation 114
greatest lower bound 30
hardware effect on time 17
hash code 156
heapsort 138, 89
hierarchical data model 196
independent access 68
least upper bound 30
lifo 41, 53
linking,address calc. 156
list 38, 39, 75
    available space 168
    circular 80
    ground 76
    one-way 76
    one-way circular 81
    one-way ground 75
    queue as a 80
    reversing linkage 78
    stack as a 77
    two-way 82
logarithmic timing 33
logical structures 2
mark procedure 172

matrix,sparse 177
measurement,space 16
measurement,time 16
merge sort 141
morse code 104
n log n timing 33
n-ary tree 45,93
n-tuple 38
network data model 208
new procedure 169
node 42
   depth of 45
   balance of 46
   child 45
   level of 45
   parent 45
   sibling 45
parity 186
path 42
   length of 42
   simple 42
physical structures 2
pointer 7
   variables 70
   child 94
   sibling 94,95,97
polygon,area of 181
   convex 183
polynomial time 31
   degree 180
   in a list 180
polyphase merge sort 145
pop 56
push 56
pushdown stack(see stack) 40
queue 39, 51,129
   double ended 41,82
   in array 51
   multiple 61
   wraparound(using) 51
quicksort 57,138
   recursive 163
   timing 57
radix sort 147
random access 37, 38, 67
record 69
records,binary tree of 92
recursion 163,164
relational data model 212
release procedure 172
root (of a tree) 44

search 151
search,address calculation 154
   bisection 152
   block sequential 158
   hash 156
   level by level tree 98
   natural order tree 97
   sequential 152
selection sort 134
sequential search 152
sequential structures 37
shell sort 135
sibling pointer 94, 95, 97
sort,address calculation 147
   bubble 134
   exchange 134
   heap 138, 89
   merge 141
   polyphase 145
   quick 138
   radix 147
   selection 134
   shell 135
   tree 138
sorting 133
space requirements 16
spanning tree 45
speed-up,graph algorithms 117
stack 40, 41, 51, 53
   as a list 77
   array (in) 53
   two in 1 array 57
storage allocation 167
storage requirements 16
structures,logical 2
   physical 2
   sequential 37
subpath 42
   proper 42
time requirements 16
   algorithm 17
   average case 31
   best case 30
   control structures 17
   data 17, 22
   hardware 17, 22
   if structure 18
   loop 17, 24
time,modularization 17, 19
time,special cases 30
time,worst case 30

timing techniques 24
    calculus 24, 27
    combinatorics 24
    graphing 24
    series summati 24, 27
    statistics 24
timing,exponential 34
    logarithmic 33
    n log n 33
    polynomial 31
    quicksort 57
tradeoffs 5
tree 44, 87
    arithmetic expression as 47
    avl 123
    balance 46,123
    balanced 88

    binary 87, 92
    dictionary 48,98
    free 44
    height of 45
    n-ary 93
    nary 45
    record representation 94
    root 44
    vector representation 129
treesort 138, 89
udpate 151
variables,pointer 70
vector 38
vector, tree in a 129
venn diagrams 187
vertex 42
wraparound 51